MW00625259

Coffin Point:

The Strange Cases of Ed McTeer, Witchdoctor Sheriff

by Baynard Woods

Published in the United States by River City Publishing
1719 Mulberry Street
Montgomery, AL 36106

Interior Designed by Lissa Monroe

Photo of Ed McTeer by Lynne Katonak

First Edition—2010

Printed in the United States of America

1 3 5 7 9 10 8 6 4 2

ISBN 13: 978-1-57966-088-8

ISBN 10: 1-57966-088-6

Library of Congress Cataloging-in-Publication Data is available.

Coffin Point

The Strange Cases of Ed McTeer, Witchdoctor Sheriff

by Baynard Woods

River City Publishing

Montgomery, Alabama

Author's Note:

Ed McTeer's long career spawned thousands of stories. This book attempts to create a cohesive narrative out of some of them. But there are plenty of McTeer stories that are not included. His own books are full of adventure and anecdote and I would urge them upon the reader. McTeer's books, however, often contradict themselves. Memory deteriorates like a corpse—as time passes, apocryphal stories proliferate just before they disappear. This book is an attempt to sort through the various stories, deal with the apocryphal, and create a coherent whole.

In writing an account of a county over the course of a century, manners of speech and spelling have changed. *Ladies Island* became *Lady's Island*. For the sake of consistency, I have regularized the spelling.

Likewise, it is now common to treat *Lowcountry* as one word. I have followed this practice everywhere, except McTeer's titles which consistently treat it as two.

One of McTeer's daughters married a Woods—but I am of no relation.

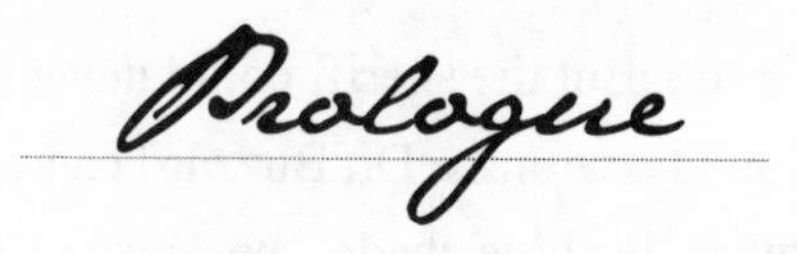

Prologue

It was time to summon Ed McTeer.

First, caretakers found voodoo dolls and strips of paper in branches hanging over a grave at the Rhett Cemetery in Beaufort County, South Carolina. Then the dead man's family noticed the dirt on his plot had been disturbed and called the authorities. A circuit court judge finally ordered the body exhumed but the cemetery's manager said, "The body didn't need to be exhumed. The grave was open, period." When investigators unlatched the coffin, they found the man's body lying there—but *only* his body. The head was missing.[1]

Sheriff Morgan McCutcheon called it the most "bizarre damn case" he'd ever seen.[2] It was 1979, and McCutcheon, a former Marine, was trying to modernize the department. This lunatic business was the last thing he needed. What was he supposed to do with hoodoo?

There was only one thing to do: Call the old sheriff, Ed McTeer, retired for sixteen years now. McTeer, a legend, was not only an expert on rootwork and witchcraft, he was a root doctor himself.

Rootwork—also called *hoodoo*, *voodoo*, and *witchcraft*—traveled with African slaves to the Lowcountry of South Carolina. McTeer, a white man, began presenting himself as a root doctor early in his long career and by the 1970s even had an office where he practiced as a "poor man's psychiatrist." Everybody had heard stories from the days when McTeer would send out word and the suspect would turn himself in, saying "Lock me up, Sheriff. Just don't do to me what you did to Dr. Buzzard."

Dr. Buzzard—whose real name was Stephaney Robinson—was the acknowledged king of the Lowcountry root doctors. Robinson had been handing out potions, which equaled practicing medicine without a license in McTeer's book. But the sheriff could never catch Dr. Buzzard. Whenever McTeer found a witness, Dr. Buzzard came into the station, flashed his fancy clothes, his blue shades, and his crooked grin. He fixed the witness with the evil eye. The witness started twitching and shaking and either refused to talk or changed his testimony. Back then, everybody in Beaufort knew snitches on witches got twitches.

Young Ed McTeer was fed up. If he couldn't defeat Dr. Buzzard within the boundaries of the law, he'd extend his jurisdiction to the spiritual realm. He began removing roots, or hexes, from people in his county. Word began to spread about McTeer. They said he practiced "white" witchcraft and called him the "White Prince." He challenged the root doctors' authority on their own turf. And why not? They were on his turf all the time, chewing roots in the courthouse, trying to affect rulings.

Dr. Buzzard declared war, making a public claim: He was going to "bring down" Sheriff McTeer.

"Tell Buzzard that trouble is close to him," McTeer responded. "I don't like to be threatened."[3]

A short time later, Dr. Buzzard's son was driving home to St. Helena's in a hotshot car. Rain beat the windshield. Lightening flashed. The roads were unpaved, the headlights dim, and the marshes beyond were flooding. Something caused Robinson's son to drive off the causeway. The vehicle sank into the marsh. Young Robinson drowned.

Admittedly, the young man drank. He'd wrecked cars before. But in the popular imagination, McTeer's magic caused young Robinson's crash. McTeer did not discourage the impression.

In one of his memoirs, McTeer wrote about coming home to find Dr. Buzzard in his driveway a short time after the wreck. Dr. Buzzard observed they both had the power; he wanted to teach McTeer the things he'd learned from his father. He agreed to quit distributing medicine and confine his business to spiritual matters.

McTeer, in turn, promised to give up "black" witchcraft. He agreed to focus on using "white" witchcraft to help people. Being accepted as a root doctor gave him the status necessary to unite the legal and spiritual authorities in Beaufort County for the next fifteen years.

At least that's the legend. And after Dr. Buzzard died, there was no one left to contradict it. McTeer, the white sheriff, was free to call himself "the last remaining tie with the true African witch doctors of the Lowcountry."

McCutcheon and his investigator must have thought of all this as they stood looking at the beheaded corpse, the strips of paper, and the voodoo dolls. If anybody could help make sense of all this, it was McTeer. Of course, they were aware how Ed McTeer loved publicity. It would be hard to keep him from talking to the press, and the papers were already going crazy. After his initial remarks, McCutcheon respected the family's wishes and refused to discuss the case at all. But sure enough, McTeer made numerous statements. By this time, he was a creepy old guy with thick glasses, long white hair and tremendous ears hanging from his skeletal head. His picture, holding voodoo dolls or amulets, was plastered across half the papers in the state with big headlines proclaiming "Lowcountry Voodoo."

McTeer told the *Beaufort Gazette* the perpetrators "went in beforehand and hung things in the trees to curse people." When that "first phase" did not prove successful "they came back and did this final thing, trying to put a spell on these people. They want to make people sick and finally to kill them." He added, "this is a true case of black magic . . . The head, they could use that to put a spell on people they're trying to kill: bury it somewhere." He went on to say that "it's kind of unusual to take parts from a body around here . . . They must have paid a great deal of money."[4]

A week later, on 29 December 1979, Ed McTeer died. Natural causes, undetermined. An old friend asked that the sheriff's office guard McTeer's corpse until it was safely interred. "Any part of his body could be extremely valuable to a voodoo practitioner," the concerned friend told McCutcheon. Finally, McTeer was buried in the cemetery of St. Helena Episcopal Church in downtown Beaufort, only a couple of blocks from the voodoo shrine in the back room of his real estate office on West Street.

The story of McTeer's battle with Dr. Buzzard cast a curious spell on me when I came across his books at my uncle's house in Hilton Head. My uncle knew a lot of people in the county; one of them put me in touch with Ed's youngest son, Thomas. Thomas McTeer worked at a used car dealership on Boundary Street in Beaufort.

I pulled into the gravel lot. Desolate cars encircled the white trailer in the center of the lot, like pilgrims praying at a shrine. The trailer's red door opened. The man who shuffled out was tall but hunched, with a boyish shock of sandy gray hair. He wore a yellow polo shirt, shorts, and flip-flops. At first I couldn't see the resemblance. Then I got out of the car and noticed that his face was heavy with exaggerated features. Something inside him was pushing outward, stretching his extremities towards some unknown goal. In the old gray photos, his father's features were stretched out in the same way. They both had the faces of men driven by disparate forces.

Thomas McTeer sized me up as we shook hands. Who the hell was this guy asking questions about his father? Not that he wasn't used to it: "My wife and I spent the first year after he died answering correspondence and cleaning off his grave, all of the things people left on it." We got in our cars and I followed him to his modest single story house, located on a marshy branch of the Pigeon Point Creek, which feeds into the Beaufort River.

The day was blazing and bright. Light entered the living room through the windows beside the fireplace and the glass door. The two shafts converged on a giant gold-painted sheriff's badge on the far wall. It read: *High Sheriff, Beaufort County, J.E. McTeer.* It was wooden, a couple of feet tall, a foot wide. Around it hung photos of the sheriff at various points in his career.

"My dad had his own museum," Thomas said. He told me the story of how the rudder indicator of the Battleship Maine—"to the family it was all one word, you know *rudderindicatorofthebattleshipmaine*"—came to reside in his living room. He pointed to a picture of his father holding a long Arabian rifle, the barrel of which widened like a phonograph. "He collected guns, among other things, and we were always told he had the second largest Colt pistol collection in existence. Colt Manufacturing being the first." Despite his extensive collection, McTeer never carried a gun as sheriff. "He carried a big flashlight and I always knew what kind of day he'd had when I'd look on his dresser and see the flashlight there with the dent in it—what kind of night he'd had. You could kind of tell if he had to use it. That was his weapon. He carried a .38 under the seat of the car but he never strapped a gun on. He was not that kind of guy. Wore a suit—law enforcement, not gun enforcement. But of course, back then sheriff was really a political position, highest in the county. Now it's not much more than a process-server."

Thomas McTeer left me looking at pictures and went to microwave us the morning's leftover coffee. In one of the pictures, two white men strode down a sidewalk in front of a white house. Both were wearing white shirts, ties, pleated pants, and fedoras. McTeer was on the right. A fish swung on a line by his side. He was laughing. The other man seemed to walk more stiffly, with a military cadence. I recognized his face. Thomas returned. "That's dad with Strom Thurmond," he said, pointing at the former Governor, Senator, and Dixiecrat presidential candidate. "That was our house on Bay Street and you see if you look up on the porch there, you can see me and my brother, Ed."

Ed, the older boy, stood bare-chested, with big-eyes and a buzz cut, a towel thrown over his shoulder, looking out at the two men. Thomas studied his own image. "I was probably three so that was '47 maybe. Probably a publicity shot or something." He took a sip from his mug. "But that was dad. He would hang out with all those political people,

Strom, Mendel Rivers, because the sheriff was the go-to guy when they needed votes," he said. "I guess they'd been fishing but I don't remember it."

He looked up with a start, as if he had forgotten something, and took another slug of coffee. "For South Carolina, Beaufort has a history of being liberal. During the early years of the Civil Rights Movement, folks like Dr. King and all knew they could come to Beaufort County because it would be safe. Dad was sworn to uphold the law but he always tried to be fair."

Thomas walked towards the couch, where his father's books and scrapbooks were laid out on the coffee table. He noticed me looking at the badge-shaped sign. "That hung outside his office. Probably made by convict labor. All that stuff was." He pointed to the wall opposite the fireplace. "That gun rack there. Well, I use it as a bookcase now, but it was made by prisoners too." He walked over to the case and knocked on the wood. "Old Pecky Cypress, real nice wood."

He told me that in the 1950s his father had been blinded by cataracts until he underwent an experimental surgery in Philadelphia. During his blindness, a convict named Albert Murray drove the sheriff around. "Albert lived in the basement of our house. We lived in the plantation house at Coffin Point and we had a room down there for Albert. He was in for murder. People used to ask me what it was like to live with a murderer in the house. I never gave it much thought. If you asked Albert why he killed his wife he would say: *Because the grits were cold. Because the grits were cold.*"

Thomas pointed over at a wooden club, two feet long, on the brick mantle. "That there is his mandrake root. He used it in his ceremonies. It's not African or anything. He had a lot of African artifacts, a whole big collection of stuff, but this was made by an old fellow that lived in a shack out on a road going towards Hunting Island and we called him Driftwood Cory. And Driftwood made this for him to use in his voodoo ritual."

He handed me the club. The wood was worn and smooth and narrow at the handle. It was top heavy and widened into a rough, horned head marked by a knotted old face with burned-on arches for eyebrows. Thomas explained the ceremony, the horseshoe crab shell, the gunpowder. He took the mandrake back and returned it to the mantle. "My mother and sisters sewed the roots," he said. "Then he'd put whatever in them. We all got one. You want to see it?" he asked.

A root is the amulet a root doctor uses to symbolize and embody the spell he casts. It is made of cloth or felt and is stuffed with a variety of poetic ingredients—roots, herbs, powders, or bones. The root that Thomas pulled from his pocket was a piece of bright blue felt about the size and shape of a ravioli. "I don't go anywhere without it," he said. He handed it to me. I studied it and gave it back to him. A mischievous glint sparkled across his deep-set dark eyes. "And without telling my mother, we did salvage some of the stuff. Let me see if I can—" He broke off mid-sentence and turned around. "Very quickly," he muttered. And then he was gone.

He went through the kitchen and opened up the attic door in the hallway and climbed the ladder, talking all the time. "I put these away. These are roots he took off of people. Roots have to have a physical quality. You can't just leave them lying around. Don't want a grandchild getting their hands on them. Could be some bad karma. Here they are," he said, finally locating a musty old briefcase hidden among old tax returns. He climbed down with it. "Prison labor made this too." He slapped the leather, sending motes of dust up through the light, then dug his hands into the bag, rustling around a minute. He brought out a root and held it up. One after another, four different roots, each a bit mustier and funkier than the last. The root made by his father looked like something a kindergarten teacher might give out as reward for good behavior, but these things were ancient, not so much dirty as chthonic, born up of the earth. They were like old hacky sacks kicked around by corpses for the last fifty years.

"So you'd find something like this under your doormat or hanging from a mailbox or buried in the yard. A root only works if you know it is there. So these are roots that people came in with for him to take the spell off. Who knows what's in these things? I mean, God knows, it's supposed to be dirt from a criminal's grave. Weird stuff like that." He put the last of the old roots back in the bag. "I do go get dirt from his grave to put in my little roots that I make."

"The roots *you* make? You make roots?"

"Just for family and friends, really," he smiled. "More or less."

After a while, Thomas said he had to get back to work. I went downtown to look at McTeer's scrapbooks in the library and make some photocopies. When I finished, I decided to go to St. Helena's Episcopal Church to see the sheriff's grave.

On the way, I walked down Bay Street to the residential area past the crisp, small town storefronts. Palatial, sun-drenched homes lined one side of the road, across from the river. I found McTeer's old address, the house where he'd been photographed with Strom Thurmond, the yard where Dr. Buzzard supposedly capitulated. I walked past and looked at the small museum he built himself out of salvaged bricks in the back yard, and on past the old courthouse, and then up to the dilapidated, art-deco jail, which Ed's brother Gerald had run for years. Bars still secured the boarded up windows. I paused for a moment and headed back towards Church Street.

When I arrived at the old church, a preppy young couple was idly reading the names and dates on gravestones, wiping sweat from their blonde foreheads. They murmured back and forth as I moved silently from plot to plot, searching for a single name. The couple eventually left, their car doors echoing from half a block away. Insects hummed. A mockingbird landed in front of me and started to strut. It hopped twice, stuck out its chest, and flew away. After forty minutes of wandering around the cemetery in the shade of old oaks that did nothing to help fight the 102 degree heat, I broke down and called Thomas to ask after the grave's location.

"You're at the church?" he asked. "There's another cemetery over across the street. Just wait right there and look for my car. I'm about to cut out to watch the Braves game that starts at three. I'll be right there."

A few minutes later, we were standing over his father's grave. "I usually find a little oyster shell to scoop the dust up with, and put the shell in my root too," he said. I knelt down. I found a shell and scraped up a bit of dirt from the grave of Ed McTeer, the white sheriff who had practiced the black arts. Thomas McTeer stood there beside me in flip-flops and shorts, watching.

It was not the "dead hour" surrounding midnight, from 11:30 to 12:30, when root doctors traditionally gather their goofer dust and cast spells. But the graveyard felt pretty dead on that August afternoon pulsing with heat, the sleepy beginning of a Braves game wafting from the window of Thomas' car up through the Spanish moss hanging from the old live oaks surrounding the cemetery.

Now, a year later, I sit trying to spell out a root with that dirt, wrapping it in the fabric of photocopies, scrawled notes, tape-recordings, photographs—all of the artifacts we secretly hope can help us raise the dead.

Chapter 2

Ed McTeer claimed he inherited a super-charged sheriff's blood from his father and ESP from his mother. These gifts guaranteed he would lead no normal life. His father, Jim Eddie McTeer, was born to a once powerful family diminished by "Reconstruction Days." Jim Eddie moved from Early Branch to Red Dam, South Carolina, where he started a business supplying cord wood and ties to the railroad.[5] He met a young woman named Florence Heyward, a descendent of Thomas Heyward, signer of the Declaration of Independence. Her family was big-time. Jim Eddie "soon discovered that W.N. Heyward considered him presumptuous to even think that he could marry into the old rice planter family . . . Jim Eddie had never attended the St. Celia Ball in Charleston."[6] Jim Eddie and Florence eloped. When her family hunted them down in an attempt to save her from the questionable McTeer, she fought back. She loved him. She didn't need rescuing. A powerful relative and future governor, Duncan Clinch Heyward, intervened. He looked at Jim Eddie and told Florence's father "this young man is the kind who will bring the South back again."[7] The young man had neither a fortune nor a pedigree, but his father-in-law learned to respect him.

Jim Eddie and Florence began to raise a family in Red Dam. Gerald, their oldest son, was born in 1896, followed by two daughters, Lila and Louisa. In 1903, James Edwin McTeer Jr. was born. Ed claimed that when he was born, the doctor declared, "Florence, I believe you have birthed a president. This boy is big, bald-headed, pompous looking, and he is already talking out of both sides of his mouth."[8]

Gerald was seven when Ed was born. Malaria hit the family hard at Red Dam, but it hit Gerald hardest. Ed wrote that it "wracked his body and sapped his strength."[9] Jim Eddie saw his oldest and strongest child sick and shivering and knew that he needed to get his family away from the miasmic fog that plagued the Lowcountry. He had a newborn child. The wealthy could afford two homes—a plantation and a summer home in some airy place with wind—Beaufort, Edisto Beach, Savannah, Charleston. But damn if Jim Eddie could afford two homes. He looked out over the land and surveyed his possibilities. He decided to go into politics. If he won, he could move his family to the county seat in Beaufort. He was going to be sheriff. It was 1904. Ed was one year old.

The incumbent, H.H. Porter, got the job when his predecessor died two years earlier, and was not especially popular. Beaufort County is big today but was even bigger back then, before Jasper County was cut out from it. Jim Eddie rode every bit of it in a buggy. He gave the voters Wyandotte chickens that Florence raised. Ed claimed that his father actually coined the phrase "a chicken in every pot."[10] But Florence didn't really have to raise enough chickens for *every* pot.

In some jurisdictions the office of sheriff is non-partisan, but in Beaufort County the sheriff's badge is forged in the primary. The population was roughly thirty-five thousand in 1900; only three thousand of those were white. African Americans were legally able to vote in South Carolina, but under the Constitution of 1895 only those who could prove they had voted for Democrat Wade Hampton in the governor's race of 1877 were allowed to vote in the state Democratic Party primaries. This insane rule kept even property-holding blacks—of whom there were many, especially on St. Helena—from voting in the only elections that mattered in the state. Women hadn't yet won the right to vote. Fewer than five percent of the population was eligible to vote for Jim Eddie McTeer.

Jim Eddie won the position. He moved his family into a home he rented in Beaufort at the corner of Charles and Craven Streets.

In town, Gerald began to recover and regain the athletic bent he had before his illness. Ed was a popular boy. He had a number of good friends. With them, he created a secret society. They called it an "Indian Gang." They ran around town, exploring, swimming, playing fox and hound, and spying on Beaufort's prominent citizens: trying at once to make sense of the adult world and to hide from it.

Of his father's work, Ed recalled a particularly vivid scene that would have a deep impact on his future. There were two trustees at the jail who "fed the dogs and kept the grounds." Deputy Danny White sometimes worked as the jailer. He found out that these guys were slipping out for a little action with their lady friends and one day he met them at the gate. "Boys, you've left this yard for the last time. I got a root powder here from Dr. Buzzard. Now you get back there and watch." Deputy White poured some white powder from a sack into the shape of a cross. "When he'd finished," McTeer wrote, "the cross stood out against the dark earth, right in the center of the gateway." The deputy told the two trustees that they could go ahead and walk right on out—but if they did, they'd never walk again. The conjugal visits ceased.[11]

This impressed Ed. The voodoo talk—and the power that came with it—added a different dimension to the spooky atmosphere of European spiritualism at home. His grandmother participated in table-tapping séances and "delved deeply into the occult." She claimed to have ESP. McTeer believed his mother Florence had inherited this power. He wrote of two separate occasions when his mother accurately dreamed of distant misfortune in the family. One morning in 1911, when Ed was seven, his mother recalled a dream to him. She saw a little girl, Ed's cousin, fall from a hammock at her brother's house in Savannah. The little girl, she dreamed, ended up with a splinter in her eye and lost it. When Florence finally saw her brother, she related the story and he said "My God Florrie, you must have been there. That's exactly what happened and our little girl lost her eye." In another instance Florence's sister Alice came to her in a dream to say goodbye. Shortly thereafter, the family got word that she had died.[12]

McTeer later reported that he inherited his mother and grandmother's extrasensory perception. He acknowledged that "I did not have the faculty which would allow me to see spirits but two of my sisters did have this ability." One sister saw "a little old lady wearing a hoop skirt and carrying an umbrella" every full moon and another "was thoroughly put out with me because I could not see the person at the graveyard she described so vividly."[13]

Chapter 3

In 1912, Deputy Matthew White defeated Jim Eddie in the Democratic Primary and took over as sheriff. Lt. Col. Neil Baxley, the unofficial historian of the Beaufort County Sheriff's Office, claims that Jim Eddie lost because the citizens were "tired of his lackadaisical approach to law enforcement." The family had no reason to remain in the County seat, and no means to. Jim Eddie was unemployed. The Indian Gang was busted up. The former sheriff moved his family to an old plantation in Grays Hill. Ed wrote that his father was a "prince of a dad" and declared that "we were a happy family on the farm."[14] But it is always hard for a nine year old boy to watch his father publicly fail.

Grays Hill was a plantation in Port Royal. It was an isolated place when the McTeers moved there in 1912. An elderly Gullah man named Tony Legare and a woman they called Aunt Emmaline were living on the farm when they arrived. The Gullah people and the Gullah language were created by the mixture of the various groups of West Africans brought to South Carolina's rice plantations from Africa's so-called "Grain Coast." The cultures and mutually unintelligible languages of Africans from Angola, Sierra Leone, the Congo, Ghana, and Gambia collided with English on South Carolina's isolated sea-island plantations and created a new culture and a new language in the New World.

McTeer wrote and spoke often about this elderly Gullah couple. He described them as the children of slaves who remained on the "land they knew" when freedom came. They lived in small cabins and did only the work necessary for their provisions. They seemed to regard the comings and goings of the white people with a bemused detachment. "Little did I know," McTeer wrote, "it would be these ancient Africans who would introduce me to African Black magic and witchcraft, and who would enlarge my vocabulary with words such as *ju-ju*, *put mout on you*, *root*, *hex,* and *spirits of the night*."[15]

McTeer told one reporter, "Witchcraft came naturally to me because I was raised on a plantation with two witchdoctors."[16] To another, he said: "On my plantation were two old black people. Their grandfathers had come from Africa as slaves. They were real witchdoctors." McTeer claimed the "witchdoctors noticed" his "power and when he was eleven, they began teaching him about roots, spells, and witchcraft."[17]

McTeer respected Aunt Emmaline but confessed that he often teased her. She only spoke Gullah and McTeer bragged that he spoke it as well as she did. He asked her when she was going to get married, to which she replied: "Hunnuh buckra chillun sho' debblish. How you tink I ga tek man wen I mos' reddy fo' de grabe yad? Yo sassy mout go cause me to put mout on you."[18]

McTeer kept teasing her, asking how she was going to "put mouth" on him when she didn't have any teeth in her gums. "I ain't put de mout on yo wit de toof. I put de mout on you wit de mout," she told him. "Ya bes' lissen or I fo' hant y' when I dead. If I put ju-ju on yo, yo gon' brek out all ovuh. I gwine mek yo' wet de bed, and yo ma wine trash yo backside. I sho gwine hant you when I gone."[19]

A nine year old boy might be expected to be afraid of wetting the bed and the whipping that would come with it, but Ed paid little attention to the threat. One night a couple of years after the old lady's death, Ed was out riding a pony. It got spooked and threw him. He came crashing down on top of the clanging dishes and pots stacked, in the Gullah tradition, on Emmaline's grave. The young boy jumped up and ran home, his steps so quickened by terror that the family joked he made it home before the horse.

He paid close attention on Sunday nights when everybody on the plantation gathered to boil cane for molasses and told stories of hags, haints, and plateyes. Tony Legare, a part time preacher, bragged that he spoke regularly with spirits of the same departed souls he had counseled while they were alive. One evening, Ed was out hunting in the graveyard, using an old felled tree as his stand. He heard Legare coming down the path, practicing a sermon in a booming voice. When Legare grew close, McTeer called out, impersonating the recently departed "Brudder Brown." Legare cried out, "great Gawd in the high heaven. The haint done got me," and ran away. Ed was learning spiritual lessons. He later claimed, "I was twelve years old when Mother told me, 'Ed, you have more sensitivity than any of your brothers and sisters. It will develop as you grow older; always use it to do good.'"[20]

Chapter 4

Ed's life was not all juju and séances. He hunted and fished, spending days at a time in the woods and waters. He and his father had to shoot his dogs when they got rabies. His mother made him empty his pockets when he came into the house each evening because of his drive to collect every oddity he found around the farm.

He started school. One teacher taught all ten grades in a single room. McTeer wrote fondly of his time at school—mainly recording pranks that he and his classmates played. They sprinkled the pollen of stinging nettles onto the seats of the "two holer" girls' outhouse and spent the rest of the day watching them squirm in their seats.

He considered his cohorts smarter than the students of the 1970s in at least one way. "Now, they have to teach them about sex in the schools. We never mentioned the word but we knew what the birds were doing. Every one of us was raised on farms which gave us a 'first hand' liberal education." He went on to recall that since they didn't have toys, the boys and girls in Grays Hill played games with names like "Doctor and Nurse, Mother and Father, Hide in the Barn, and Rooster and Hen." Ed recalled that when his father caught him playing "Hide in the Barn" with a girl in town for the weekend, he "had to really convince Dad I would run off to Canada and spend the rest of my days trapping" if Mrs. McTeer found out.[21]

The farm was good for Gerald, too. He was bursting with health. At eighteen he went to a boxing match at the Beaufort Armory. A sweaty crowd was gathered and ready for a heavy weight fight. But one of the contenders didn't show. The crowd started hollering. The announcer asked if anyone from the audience wanted to come up to the ring and give it a go. Gerald was a big guy and his friends started egging him on.

He got up and climbed into the ring. The boxer whispered to Gerald, telling him not to worry, he'd take it easy. Gerald replied, "I'm here to fight. You do your best." Gerald knocked the guy out before the end of the third round. On the basis of this win, Gerald went into training. The regimen was good for him. He got stronger and better. He started fighting in Florida. He kept winning fights, until he joined the 10th Aero Squadron when the U.S. finally entered the Great War.[22]

According to Ed, Gerald was "a master aviation mechanic." He was shot down and spent several months in a French hospital, then sailed home from Le Havre on a ship named *Espagne*. The records at Ellis Island show he landed on 15 July 1919. There is no other record of Gerald's homecoming, but the hero of Ernest Hemingway's story "Soldier's Home" also returned from the war in the summer of 1919. "By the time he returned to his home town . . . the greeting of heroes was over. He came back much too late. The men from the town who had been drafted had all been welcomed elaborately on their return. There had been a great deal of hysteria. Now the reaction had set in. People seemed to think it was rather ridiculous . . . to be getting back so late, years after the war was over."[23]

Gerald was never able to recover from his physical injuries, and they brought back the old, general ill health that had plagued him in childhood. After his return "pleurisy and numerous other ailments beset him. Many times death was at his bedside, but a little flicker of life kept him going," Ed wrote. He added with sadness that his brother was a "shadow" of his old self. Gerald took to drinking; his muscle became fat; he floundered.[24]

Ed was fourteen when Gerald came home. Ed witnessed his brother's suffering and the lost-ness of that generation. But Ed was not lost. He was thriving. The school board had closed the school in Grays Hill. Jim Eddie bought a tarpaulin covered truck to serve as a school bus; Ed drove the truck and hauled all the Grays Hill kids to Beaufort High School in town.

Ed was popular with girls and boys, teachers and adults. He hunted and fished. He played football, chased girls, and farmed. He played guitar and mandolin in a little string band. His father played poker on Friday nights, leaving Ed with the car until 11:00, when he would pick up the old man. If Jim Eddie was losing, he might keep Ed waiting until three in the morning. That didn't mean the kid could keep the girl out that long. If Jim Eddie was winning, he couldn't get outside quick enough and Ed needed to be there when he did.[25]

When Ed graduated and walked across the stage, everyone was sure that he would really be something.[26] But he wasn't anything. At least not yet. The economy started to tank in the Southern states just as he graduated. He wanted to go to Clemson. He was intensely curious, and he could talk. He knew the law well from watching his father's career and had long wanted to be a lawyer. But his family couldn't afford it. He stuck around town, farming with Jim Eddie for a while. In 1918 the family was offered $125,000 for the farm. By 1924, the bank was threatening to foreclose.[27] It was a bad time. They were all hungry, but Ed was starving with the brutal self-masticating hunger that the inexperienced and young know so well. He wanted the world.

Chapter 5

As Ed was trying to figure out what to do with his life, Jim Eddie was rethinking his own. The farm wasn't going to make him money and he'd be lucky not to lose it. He decided to run for sheriff again. Matthew White, in office since he beat Jim Eddie back in 1912, had been extremely popular. But in 1920, White got sick and died. A deputy finished his term but lost the office to James Bailey that same year.

Bailey was a tough customer. He had a wide face, thick white hair and a long white mustache—like Mark Twain but meaner. His face looked hard and ornery with eyes used to squinting in the sun. The sheriff was low-paid and had to make money in other ways. Some of that was accepted. But Bailey's term seemed a little too lucrative for hard times. Jim Eddie thought he had a chance to take the badge back.

At the end of 1925, Jim Eddie McTeer defeated Bailey. By the time his father retook office early the following year, Ed had moved to Baltimore. One of his friends had a brother who worked for the electrical company up there who said he could get them training and a job. Ed and his friend packed up and moved to the city that H.L. Mencken described as a "wicked seaport" with the odor of "a billion pole cats." Even without the polecats, Baltimore had a population of 750,000 people. And they were there in the middle of it.

They worked with the future: electricity. The very thought was exciting. Sure, there was electricity in the town of Beaufort; the city government controlled the utility, but it was highly unreliable. It flashed in and out. It was unpredictable, almost useless. But people loved it. They desired it. They felt stranded when it was gone. Nothing creates a drive for power like impotence and Beaufort's spotty power grid showed everyone just how powerful the electric world would be. They needed young men like Ed to go out, learn electrical engineering, and come back home to act as priests to this new Zeus.

While Ed was in Baltimore, the Philadelphia Electric Company produced a film called *All the King's Horses*, which captured the attitude of the age. It began with the title "Primitive Man" and showed a caveman watching horses run. He dreamed of harnessing their power. But when people finally managed to capture that power it was monopolized by kings and tyrants . . . "until now." Now, the Philadelphia Electric Company declared: "These great hydroelectric units together with steam plants turn great machines and presto! The magic of electricity leaps to the service of all the people."

Images of power plants and turbines rocked the movie screen. Warbling text followed: "Intricate networks of wires and cables carry the mysterious power of the modern world everywhere . . . Through giant cables and tiny wires, in the air and underground, the mysterious forces of electrical energy—like a thundering herd—flow constantly toward the service of the people."[28] This could really draw in a young man looking to experience the world. Electricity was the new magic.

In 1925, Ed's employer, the Consolidated Gas Electric Light and Power Company of Baltimore, "completed the first part of a high voltage ring around the city to improve electric distribution."[29] McTeer, dressed in coveralls, goggles and a hard-hat, "soon became a trouble shooter, taking all the dangerous and difficult assignments for the power firm."[30]

Meanwhile, the Scopes Trial in Tennessee brought national attention to regional differences. The "Sage of Baltimore," H.L. Mencken, was covering the Evolution trial for the *Evening Sun*. Walking the streets, Ed could surely hear the paper boys cry out the headlines. Mencken was known for his wit, and now it was often focused on the South, McTeer's home. In one essay, Mencken called the Carolinas "a vast plain of mediocrity, stupidity, lethargy, almost of dead silence."[31] But Ed's own wit was quite sharp and he was never silent. He could hold his own with anyone who quipped about his accent.

1926 promised to start like a restoration for Jim Eddie. He was preparing to make a triumphant return to office. At that time, the sheriff had a deputy or two, but there was also a system of rural policemen working throughout the county. These rural policemen answered to the County Board but worked closely with the sheriff. On January 6, just before Jim Eddie resumed his old office, Deputy Hubert Randall and Rural Policeman Paul Carden drove out to Seabrook to make an arrest. Two brothers, Willie and Ben Heyward, had gotten into trouble. Carden and Randall went to bring them in. They parked the car and got out and walked up to the door of the "negro shack." Carden knocked. The officers identified themselves. From inside, one of the two brothers opened fire with a shotgun. He shot Carden right through the door. Carden fell back in a slump of gore. Randall picked him up. The brothers kept shooting. One called Carden's name and fired. Randall rushed his wounded colleague to the car. Bullets struck the automobile with the slapping sound of bent metal. Randall got down behind it, opened the door, and got Carden in. Blood poured into the floorboard. Randall drove away, still under fire.

Paul Carden died. The county was outraged. Jim Eddie took the oath of office a few days later.

Race relations were tense. A decade earlier, in 1915, Constable Cooler, the brother of a rural policeman was assassinated while on a liquor bust at a blind tiger (an illegal distributor of alcohol) on St. Helena. It almost tore the county apart. The Klan was resurging at the time. It was clear that black bootleggers had killed Cooler. There were still plenty of Confederate veterans alive. It looked like the delicate social fabric would come unwound. Then police captured the killer. He was tried, convicted, and sentenced to death. Rural Policeman Cooler, the brother of the slain constable, took the convicted man to prison in Columbia, where he was hanged. Outright disaster was averted. There were no lynchings. There were no riots. But there was little hope of racial harmony. The decade simmered. And now, the Heyward brothers killed Carden and escaped clean. The most publicly scrutinized test of Jim Eddie would be his ability to find the killers.

But he never did. In the first few cold days of 1926, the sheriff went to make a late night arrest in an old topless Ford. It started raining. He caught pneumonia. He died five days later, at 1:30 on a Wednesday afternoon. The town was shocked. Hadn't they just seen him out on the streets?

The county found itself yet again without a sheriff. The family was devastated. There were still several girls and the youngest boy, Zeke, at home. What were they going to do? Gerald wasn't able to help much and Zeke was too young. And Ed was away, up North. Florence grieved and fretted for the future of her family.

Despite his promising position, Ed quit his job. He said whatever goodbyes he needed to say in Baltimore and returned home to Beaufort by train. His father, Jim Eddie, was buried at 11:00 on Thursday morning, February 4, at St. Helena's Episcopal. Ed assumed responsibility for the family—and the shaky mortgage on the farm. A week later, on 11 February 1926, Ed McTeer was appointed to fill his father's term as sheriff. He was twenty-two years old.

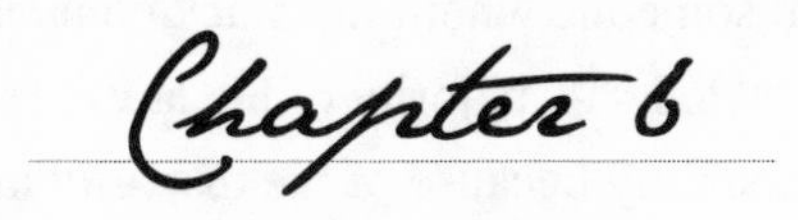

Why did the governor appoint as sheriff a twenty-two year old kid who had been living in Baltimore and working as an electrical engineer? The last half-century had seen numerous Beaufort sheriffs die in office. In most of these cases, the coroner filled the remainder of the dead man's term. The coroner was rather aged when Jim Eddie died, but there were deputies and the rural policemen already familiar with the demands that came with policing the area. Deputy Hubert Randall had just been ambushed. He had performed heroically and tried to save his fallen colleague. Deputy Cooler had escorted the men who killed his brother to the penitentiary in Columbia, where they were eventually executed. Why would the governor choose McTeer over men such as these?

I decided to go and talk to Lt. Col. Neil Baxley of the Beaufort County Sheriff's Office. Baxley is the author of a book on the Civil War and an unpublished true crime book about a Beaufort County murder. Then he started writing a history of Beaufort County through the lens of its Sheriff's Office; for the last six years, he had spent his evenings reviewing old issues of the *Beaufort Gazette* on the microfilm machine at the library.

When I called him on the phone he was delighted to talk about the events of 1926. He told me to come by the Department and he would share some files. When I arrived, he was sitting behind his desk, stuffed manila files spread out on top. He had short red hair. His quick and steady eyes revealed the curiosity that made him a good researcher and investigator. When I asked him why he thought the Governor would have appointed Ed to be sheriff he said that the black population had supported the elder McTeer. "Race has got to have played a part," he said. The Beaufort delegation in the state legislature and the local authorities were going to "want someone whom the black community would either respect or fear," he added. "A majority of his law enforcement encounters would be black, simply because of the disparity in population." The Heyward brothers were still at large. Tension was high on both sides of the color line. He could appear neither too lenient nor too hostile. Perhaps this is why Randall and Cooler were passed over. They were both so personally involved in difficult interracial cases. They might have been seen by the blacks as immediately and irrevocably biased.

Whatever the reasoning, within a week, Ed's appointment had been announced. He told different stories to reporters over the years. In one version, Governor McLeod called the young McTeer before him. "McLeod opened the conversation by saying, 'I've been talking with some men from Beaufort and they tell me they think you'd make a mighty fine sheriff. I want you to know what a terrible responsibility I am taking upon my shoulders. If I do this, you'll be the youngest sheriff in the state, maybe the nation.'"[32]

In another version of the story, McTeer himself went to the governor and asked to be made sheriff. The governor told McTeer that a single mistake by such a young sheriff could ruin the governor who appointed him. According to McTeer, the Governor then asked: "What would you do if you had a prisoner and a mob threatened to take him from you?" McTeer answered that he would stop them.

"And what if they attacked you?"

Ed replied, "I would keep shooting as long as the bullets lasted."[33]

The *Beaufort Gazette* expressed confidence in the young man, writing, "It is believed, from what we have heard of him, he will make Beaufort a good sheriff, following in the footsteps of his father." But the local wags wondered if the "Boy Sheriff"—as they dubbed him—was up to the job.

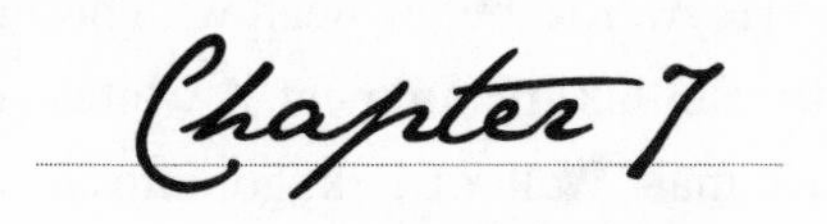

Ed McTeer wrote that the "new gold badge gleaming and all the girls fluttering their eyes at the youngest sheriff in the United States" made up for the small salary.[34] Ed had a reputation as a ladies' man. Soon, local big shots recruited him to bring imported showgirls out to Pleasant Point Plantation on Lady's Island. People say there was an indoor pool out there with a trapeze mounted above it where the dancers would swing.

Ed may have been having fun but he inherited a chaotic office. It was hard enough for a twenty-two year old with no law enforcement experience to win the respect of old timers like Cooler and Randall, but the authority of various offices was not clearly defined. The rural policemen answered to the County Board but helped the sheriff run the jail and the chain gang.

The jail was over forty years old. An inspection that year said it was "of an antique type."[35] There were no facilities for women. The jailor also served as a deputy. When he was away, his wife ran the jail. When Ed took office, he managed to build a kitchen and a dining hall on the premises. He installed toilets in the quarters and a shower outside. There were no screens for either the shower or the windows and of course there was no air conditioning. Still, he managed to make significant improvements. The chain gang did exceptionally good work when they were building their own facilities.

The county generally had three ten-man work crews. The inspector noted excellent discipline on the chain gang. All of the prisoners were trustees. Perhaps McTeer had recalled Deputy White's method of managing trustees and used his words: "I've got a root powder here from Dr. Buzzard . . . If you want to go out again, just walk across this line, but if you do, you'll never walk again."[36]

He didn't find the Heywards, but he dealt with his first interracial murder just a month after his appointment. A white man named W.F. Slowman and a black man, Walter Clark, got into an argument in Bonny Hall, about twenty miles from town. Clark threatened to go to the new sheriff with a complaint about Slowman. Slowman got in his car and sped away as fast as an old Ford could scoot across those unpaved roads. Clark took off in the same direction, but stopped on the side of the road to pick up two other black men who needed a ride. The three men were talking as Slowman pulled up. He got out of the car with his rifle and raised it. The two witnesses reported that Slowman said "You will never have handcuffs put on me," before firing his rifle through Clark's windshield. Clark cried out "You've shot me. Don't shoot anymore." Slowman tried to shoot again but his gun was empty. Clark picked up his own gun and shot Slowman. Slowman dropped his rifle, walked fifty yards and fell down dead. Clark bled to death in his automobile.[37]

There was nothing to investigate or solve. There was no way to make it right, just shattered families in a fragile community, mourning. Many whites in the county were angered when a black man killed a white man under any circumstances, even if he was defending himself. Especially after Carden. More people wondered if the "Boy Sheriff" could handle the job.

Chapter 8

On 20 April 1926, the State Attorney General determined that "the governor had no right to appoint McTeer for the full unexpired term." Ed would have to run in the primary and general election that year. Within the month, two other candidates announced for sheriff. Cooler, the brother of the slain constable, and W.F. Sanders, a former Mayor and County Supervisor, were both ready to take Ed's place.

On 10 July, just six weeks before the primary, the Bank of Beaufort, one of the town's two banks, closed unexpectedly. Half of the county's liquid assets were gone. Individuals and businesses lost savings, checking and credit accounts. The county sunk in chaos. People wanted stability. But things were changing and they needed someone who could steer them ahead, someone with a vision for the future.

A prominent citizen named W.M. DeLoach joined the race for Sheriff. At the stump meeting a week before the August primary, DeLoach called the position "one of the highest gifts the citizens of the county could bestow." He promised to undertake the duty with the seriousness it required. He said he had searched his soul before deciding to run. He had been a friend of Ed's father. The county needed firm leadership and law enforcement.

Cooler reminded voters of the well-loved Sheriff White for whom he had worked. He had experience. When his brother was assassinated, he delivered the guilty culprits to prison in Columbia without harming them—an act honest and upstanding, not to mention tragic. He deserved to be sheriff.

Sanders asked the voters to recall his long and distinguished career: He'd been in politics almost as long as the "Boy Sheriff" had been alive. He'd served a four-year stint as Mayor and eighteen years as County

Supervisor. Not only that, but, unlike this kid, old W.F. Sanders was personally virtuous. McTeer later wrote that "Sanders proceeded to elaborate his qualifications for Sheriff: He never cursed or smoked, never visited a house of pleasure, never gambled, and never had a drop of liquor passed his lips."[38]

McTeer told Sanders he had ended up at the wrong meeting. "If he hurried he could still make it to the preachers' convention." Then he asked, "If Sanders had never partaken of life, how could he be qualified to catch a wrong-doer?"[39]

The *Gazette* reported that McTeer had to respond to another charge. "He denied allegations made that he was 'appointing a bunch of young men to act as his deputies.'" McTeer said he would run on the record of his first seven months in office.[40] He *had* hired his brother, Gerald McTeer, the wounded veteran home from the Great War.

When the Democratic Party primary came on 31 August, only 1,153 votes were cast. McTeer later claimed that the other candidates thought no one would win on the first ballot. The losers would urge their supporters to vote for Ed's opponent in the run-off. McTeer's 618 votes beat all the other candidates combined, on the first ballot. The *Gazette* reported that "DeLoach and Cooler ran close for a poor second." And Sanders? He brought in seventy-four votes.

Ed had his first taste of politics.

Having won an election, McTeer had four years to make some changes. Four years was a long time for a twenty-three year old. White men elected him, but he knew that his true success would depend on his interactions with the black community. He later wrote that he began building an "extensive collection of African works" by colonial authors like "Selous, Grant, Speke, and Burton, not to mention a score of others." Ed wrote that Africa "first interested, then fascinated me, and I read everything I could get my hands on."[41]

A reporter later summarized Ed's thinking at the time: "Since Negroes made up nearly half the population, he felt he needed to understand them in order to render fair, effective law enforcement."[42]

Ed wrote of an encounter during his first year in office: "I had the occasion to be riding with an old Beaufort citizen who held the office of coroner." The coroner was the second-most powerful county-wide position and often filled in for the sheriff in an emergency. This old Beaufort citizen may well have been unhappy to have been passed over in favor of this young kid. They were driving to investigate a death and couldn't find the right house. When they saw two black women on the side of the road, they stopped to ask for directions.

As they pulled up, the coroner assured the sheriff that he knew just how to talk to the women. He told Ed, "To get information out here, you have to talk in their language." McTeer certainly agreed "that in order to get information from a person you had to . . . speak to him on his own level." But he understood that the "hard part is finding the level before speaking."[43]

McTeer recorded the conversation between the coroner and the women: "'Ebenin',' the coroner said as he rolled down his window. 'Yo' all ain' no weh brudder Steben Small house is, enty?'"

McTeer continued, dryly: "The women stared at him as if he were crazy." Then one of them said to the other, "I don't know to what or to whom he's alluding, do you, Celia?" The other woman replied "No, Jane . . . I believe the man's insane."

When one of the women asked McTeer if he knew what his companion was talking about, the young sheriff shook his head, as if he thought the old man crazy. McTeer asked for the information in plain English.

Over time, McTeer developed his own ideas about race. He told a reporter that "violence among ignorant negroes stems from a heightened instinct for self preservation—carried over from the jungle. . . . In Africa men fought nature and each other. Death or slavery was just around the corner. Cruelty was a way of life."

Chapter 10

At that time the city of Beaufort was debating whether to cede control of the city's power to the Edisto Public Works Company. McTeer may have thought back to his old friends in Baltimore; it had been less than a year since he left them. He had just won his first election and was sheriff of this crazy county. What could the roughneck linemen and big city girls in Baltimore think about that? City people didn't know about sheriffs. They knew police, but there's a big difference between the two. McTeer recalled, "In 1926, the sheriff of a small county was an important person. Every facet of the citizens' lives were brought to his doorstep. Only felony cases were brought before a judge."[44]

But Ed wanted still more power. He thought the rural police system was inefficient. It did not make sense for the County Board to have its own police force. He tried to prove the "limitations of the system."[45] But the County Board didn't want to cede its authority over county policing. The 1895 state constitution gave most of each county's authority to its delegation at the state house in Columbia. The power over the rural police was among the only real powers the County Board retained.

Ed attended his first South Carolina Sheriff's Association Convention in 1926. None of the sheriffs liked the rural police force. Ed was by far the youngest sheriff there. The difference between him and the older men was immediately obvious. Sheriff Bailey, who lost the election to Ed's father two years earlier, fit the mold much better. These were old guys with big hats, big mustaches, and big guns. Ed was young, tall, and thin, with a clean-shaven face and slicked back hair. He wore a conservative suit. He didn't wear a big six shooter on his hip.

McTeer had told the Governor that he'd keep firing into a mob until he was out of bullets, but a year in office had changed his mind. One night,

McTeer was out with Rural Policeman Langford to bust a liquor still. According to McTeer, he and Langford were waiting in the woods as two black men approached. One carried a gun and gave orders to the other, who carried an axe. McTeer overheard their conversation.

"I heah dat de elec' a boy fo' sheriff," one man said. The other said it was good because it would take a boy a long time to learn the job.

"But he got dat Langford to teach 'um, an' he can learn 'im fast," the first responded.

"Yeah, dat boy fadder been a good man, but he too ole to lay up in de woods an' bodder us. I reckon we got to watch dis young 'un. Dis sheriff, dey say he full of fire."[46]

According to the sheriff, the moment they mentioned *fire*, Langford jumped up, cocked his pistol, and hollered for the men to freeze. One guy dove for his rifle. The other kicked out the fire: chaos, sparks and blackness. Then a shot rang out. Langford yelled out that he had been hit. The young sheriff fired at the fleeing men. With every shot he heard one of the men shout out. Then there was silence. McTeer was certain he'd shot at least one of them. He walked over to Langford who was repeating, "I'm shot" over and over again. McTeer told him it would be all right. Langford said: "I shot myself." His voice full of shame, he explained that his own pistol went off when he grabbed for the man with the gun. "I think I've blown my thumb off," he said. The sheriff looked at the older man's hand. "No question about his statement. His thumb was gone."[47]

McTeer found the bootleggers that evening. Both had been scratched up by the briars during their escape, but neither had been shot. The sheriff was relieved. McTeer learned something that night. He was typically a good shot and kept in practice, hunting and fishing. He was building up a gun collection, but on the job he kept his gun under the seat of his car. At that Sheriff's Convention, he got a new nickname to go along with "Boy Sheriff," as if that wasn't bad enough: "Sheriff without a gun."

McTeer explained that "back then, the sheriff had to go on every call, personally investigate every crime, and personally make the arrests and settle the disputes. What good would a single pistol have done me in the midst of a crowd of two hundred people?" He went on to say that "after a while I found that I simply didn't need a gun, and accomplished much more without one."[48]

That was hard for people to see. Randolph Murdaugh, the Circuit Court Solicitor in Beaufort told a television crew: "First time I found out he didn't use a gun when he was investigating cases, particularly bad cases like murder cases or some cases where they were apt to have violence if the person was arrested, I asked him why he didn't carry a gun. He said he'd never run into anybody in his life he couldn't talk them into doing what he wanted them to do. Some of the worst murder cases we ever had in this county and he'd go out and arrest the people and never have a gun, a billy stick, or anything with him. He was the most articulate individual. He could talk you into doing anything."[49]

Meanwhile, as he took a break one day and was sitting out on the park bench he called the "Buzzard's Roost" where the wind from the bay created "pleasurable havoc" on the skirts of passing women, Ed noticed a beautiful young woman he'd never seen before. [50] Her dress cut a stark pattern against the pearly sky. He asked around and discovered that she was a Home Economics teacher named Ms. Lucille Lupo. She'd just moved into town from Dillon to take the job. Ed liked the way Ms. Lupo looked, short and small, quite a contrast to his athletic lankiness. Eventually his power of persuasion earned himself a date.

The bridge that was currently—it seemed interminably—being built between Beaufort and Lady's Island stood out there over the river half-completed like a promise. The present, it seemed, was always a half finished bridge reaching out into emptiness between two worlds.

On Halloween Day 1926, Rural Policeman Langford was taking a drive with his family on the road between Beaufort and Yemasee, his hand still bandaged. Fall was beautiful in Beaufort as the air softened and the leaves began to change on the smaller trees, providing furtive flashes of crisp color between the branches and leaves of the evergreen live oaks and the gray lace of Spanish moss. They passed a group of people on the side of the road near some picnic grounds. One black man and two black women flagged down the policeman. Langford reported that when he got out of the car to investigate, the man, William Maxwell, appeared obviously drunk. According to police reports, Maxwell pulled a pistol and threatened to shoot Langford in front of his wife and children. Langford eased his way into his car and took off. He looked in the rear-view mirror as he drove away.

Langford took his family home and recruited Ed's former opponent William DeLoach, whom he deputized, along with another man. He picked up a city police officer on the way out. The four men armed themselves with rifles and shotguns and took a car to Maxwell's house. Langford sent DeLoach and the other man to cover the back door. He and the city police officer remained up front. Langford yelled into the house and told Maxwell that he'd better come on out. According to Langford, Maxwell started firing at him. That was it. All four white men began shooting into the house. Through the air, the bullets came like sparrows. Maxwell may not have known that the back door was covered, because he burst out and tried to flee. When he found himself under fire by DeLoach and the other man, Maxwell darted back into the house.

Over fifty shots were fired into the home. When Maxwell would not come out, Langford decided to set the house on fire. Burn him out. One of the other men, a big guy, thought he could bust the front door down. He flung himself against it and the door burst open. Maxwell tried to flee out the back again. Already wounded, he was shot in the hip when he got out the door. His bone shattered, he fell onto his face, and was shot again, arrested, brought to the "negro infirmary" and locked up.[51]

That didn't help race relations a bit. Nor did it quell the questions of whether the "Boy Sheriff" really was up to this kind of job. He'd run strong in the election, but there was a steep learning curve, and he was still making mistakes. McTeer wrote of a time during that first year when he was sent up to New York with extradition papers for a Mr. Blethers who had been charged with desertion and non-support of his wife.

Though Ed had lived in Baltimore the previous year, he'd forgotten how cold it could be up North. When he got to Albany, McTeer wrote, he immediately bought an overcoat to keep warm. It didn't quite fit and Ed felt ramshackle and out of place. When he went to the jail, he felt they were reluctant to trust him with the prisoner.

Though Blethers was a former Marine, by this time, McTeer described him as pleasant, portly, and old. McTeer was confident of his own strength and speed and he uncuffed Blethers for the train trip. They stopped for the night in New York City and instead of locking up the man, Ed shared his own room at the New Yorker Hotel and took the prisoner to see a show. On the way out of the theater, Ed turned and found that the prisoner was gone. He frantically searched the city to no avail. He finally returned to the room, defeated. He was ready to call the police department for help. He was embarrassed and humiliated. He'd really botched this. Maybe this wasn't for him after all, despite his sheriff's blood.

He made it back to 34th and 7th and went into the hotel. He opened the door to his room and found his prisoner waiting there for him. The man told the young sheriff that he'd been wondering where he had gone. He was about to call the police to look for him.[52]

Ed McTeer made it home with the prisoner and nobody needed to know the story of how he was almost lost, until years later, when McTeer could safely laugh at himself and his youthful mistakes. At the time, he'd started to realize that he would be as effective as people thought he was. His badge was a kind of root. If people believed in its authority, then it was there. The minute they quit believing in it, it ceased to function.

Chapter 12

McTeer was just getting started, but Dr. Buzzard was already a legend. McTeer heard that Dr. Buzzard got his mantle, or powers, either from his father, or grandfather, who had been a powerful rootworker in Africa. He had also heard that Dr. Buzzard got the "sight" when a mockingbird came down and landed on his head.[53]

But Dr. Buzzard is an old name with a long tradition. Caroline Long, archivist and author of *Spiritual Merchants*, placed the earliest reference to Dr. Buzzard in 1893. The name appeared again in the memoir of Mamie Gavin Fields, who claimed to have first heard of Dr. Buzzard in 1909. Even then he was called the "witchdoctor of witchdoctors."[54] The most numerous early references appear in Harry Middleton Hyatt's *Hoodoo-Conjuration-Witchcraft-Rootwork*. Long correctly reports that Hyatt's groundbreaking book is full of "fantastic and wildly conflicting stories about Dr. Buzzard," the most bizarre of which present Dr. Buzzard as a white man living out near Florence, South Carolina. Of the white Dr. Buzzard an informant said, "He was a natural white man. But he was wonderful."[55]

Another informant told Hyatt that he had known the white Dr. Buzzard since 1908. But, the informant also said he knew of Robinson who "is down there now." When Hyatt asked if Dr. Buzzard was still living, the informant answered: "He's not daid. No sir, he ain't. No sir, Ah mean he ain't daid. Down there tuh Beaufort. He ain't daid. Dere's one dere dat dey calls Dr. Buzzard but he ain't Doctor Buzzard. He's a man. Dat Dr. Robertson. You can call him Dr. Buzzard, but if you do he won't even recognize you. Dr. Robertson."[56]

Caroline Long found Stephaney Robinson, the most famous Dr. Buzzard, in the census of 1880 when he was "a young boy living with his parents." Thomas Robinson, Stephaney's father, was not a witchdoctor from Africa, as the legend had it, but a native of South Carolina. Long also notes that in 1910 and 1920 Robinson was listed as "living with his wife Molcey and their many children."[57]

Ed, too, fell to the spell of love as he continued to court Lucille, the Home Economics teacher. By the time classes finished that summer, the two were planning to elope. Somehow, word of their elopement leaked out and Ed's mother convinced them to be married at St. Helena Episcopal. The ceremony was on Friday 3 June 1927. Ed's brother Gerald and his sister, now Mrs. George Crocker, stood as witnesses in the old white church house downtown. The bride was described as petite, "attractively gowned in blue flat crepe, fashioned with the new cape effect, with hat and accessories to match. She carried a huge bouquet of Killarney roses."[58]

Ed's mother held a reception and a buffet dinner for the newlyweds after the ceremony. The "lovely home was attractively and simply decorated with pink and white oleanders and pink tapers softened the shadow glow on the room." The cake "was placed among Shasta daisies and ferns" as a centerpiece. Ed's sisters served the buffet and "presided over" the punch bowls.[59]

After the dinner, everyone wished the young sheriff and his new bride well as they hoisted themselves into his Ford and began the long drive north to Dillon, where the Lupo family operated a large tobacco farm. The newlyweds would spend a couple of days there with the bride's family. Surely the county could survive for a couple days without its "Boy Sheriff."

On Monday morning, while Ed was still in Dillon, two men coming into Beaufort from Savannah were sideswiped by another car. Langford took the call. He had no luck tracking the reckless drivers down and went out to Combahee on other business with a friend named McDaniel. On his way back to town, Langford saw an auto matching the description from the hit and run in Grays Hill, not far from the sheriff's farm.

Langford slowed down and noticed a group of "negroes" having a picnic and throwing around a baseball.

He stopped and identified the car's driver—a man named Frank Francis. Langford moved to arrest him. Francis resisted "and caught Langford in the collar." Langford hit Francis with his pistol. Francis' father, Paul, stepped behind Langford and shot him in the back. Langford fell. McDaniel pulled out a derringer and shot Frank Francis. He tried to use his second shot on Paul, but the gun jammed. Paul fired on McDaniel, who dove into the car. McDaniel fled, leaving Langford lying there beside the field.[60]

When McDaniel reached town, Gerald McTeer took charge of the response. He gathered DeLoach and several others and raced to the crime scene. They were horrified by what they found when they arrived in Grays Hill. Langford was dead. He was lying there in a pool of blood and gore. The perps had crushed his skull and shot him twice in the back. Twice in the hands, too, mocking the accident that blew off his thumb. They stabbed him in the chest so many times the wounds blended together into a bloody mess. Eight sets of teeth marks ripped the skin down his arm.

Mobs of white men gathered across the county, searching for the suspects. Gerald sent out a wire for an APB, state-wide and down into Georgia. The Francises were heading for Savannah when a group of white men overtook them in Ridgeland. Frank Francis was leaking blood badly where the bullet hit him. They left him in custody at the hospital in Ridgeland. Six others were brought to Beaufort, locked up, and charged with murder. One man was still missing.

When word reached Dillon, the newlywed sheriff cut short his honeymoon and tore back across the state to make it home in time for Langford's funeral at Beaver Dam.

As the Circuit Court convened that summer, the judge made some opening remarks in which he attributed the "Great Crime Wave" in Beaufort to racial disparity. "White men could play poker all night unmolested," he said. "But a negro gets several years for a small craps game."

These remarks couldn't begin to address what was about to happen in Beaufort.[61]

Ed McTeer went down to Columbia to pick up six of the eight suspects. He was to bring them back to Beaufort for trial. Governor Richards declared, "There will be no lynching." He called two National Guard machine gun units to escort McTeer and the prisoners to Beaufort. When they got there, McTeer asked the unit to set up on the roof of the antiquated jail. People could clearly see them on top of the art-deco building on King Street. McTeer told the *Gazette* they set up with "machine guns, rifles, pistols, tear gas and grenades." If all that couldn't prevent a lynching, Ed figured, nothing would.[62]

The next day, June 28, a deputy from Savannah called and told Ed that two hundred blacks would arrive in Beaufort by boat at two that afternoon. The sheriff conferred with the chief of police and the major in charge of the Guard unit. They decided that they were going to "take no chances for any trouble while the negroes who killed Policeman Langford are in jail." They surrounded the craft at the dock, and McTeer and his deputies went aboard. They searched all two hundred passengers, found a few bottles of whiskey, but no weapons, and allowed the group to disembark.[63]

At the trial, Paul Francis, Frank Francis, and Abraham Gadsen were convicted of murder, with no recommendation for mercy. They were sentenced to death. Ethel Francis and Robert Adams were convicted of murder with a recommendation of mercy. They received life in prison. Another man was found guilty of manslaughter.

The next week, the bridge to Lady's Island opened. It was the first bridge to connect South Carolina's sea islands with the mainland. The *Gazette* reported, "Colored people make great showing in formal opening of the bridge." Times were hard and the bridge meant that the Gullah people on the islands could go elsewhere to look for work. But not everyone was happy about it. Some thought the Lady's Island Bridge was the beginning of the end of the Gullah way of life. Still, as he patrolled the site of the celebration, things seemed better to Ed McTeer. He might have gotten a few hard-eyed stares, but the Gullah people who were barbecuing and laughing all waved and smiled. Things almost seemed like they might get back to normal.

When Ed went home to Lucille that night he had reason to believe that they'd weathered the storm. He'd prevented both lynching and riot. He once said you had to be "half alligator, half duck to do the job," but the bridge would bring everything closer. It would make the County easier to control. [64] If things went well, maybe Ed and Lucille could even find the time to pick up where they left off on their honeymoon.

McTeer stayed home late that next Saturday morning. He got a call at 11:00 a.m. A white woman out in Hardeeville had allegedly been raped by a black man. Ed later wrote that the Hardeeville policeman who called to tell him about the rape warned that "the entire countryside" was looking for the rapist. "His voice," McTeer wrote, "was urgent and worried." The officer feared there would be a lynching. If they didn't catch the assailant and found another black man, the officer told the sheriff, they might lynch him instead.[65]

The victim said she had been lying in bed asleep after her husband left for work. Her small children were sleeping in the other room. Two black men crawled in through the window, waking her. She pleaded with them. One of the men, she said, left in peace, but the other pulled out a "switchback" knife and put it to her throat. He raped her, she said, as her children cried at the door, then escaped through the window. She climbed out after him, crying and disheveled, to try and get a better look at her assailant.

McTeer called the Chatham County Sheriff's office to request their bloodhounds "Music" and "Red." By the time the dogs got to the scene, the tracks were over eight hours old and the dogs could not get a trail. On his way to the scene Ed saw a large group of men gathered and he pulled his car to the side of the road. "The first thought that entered my mind was that Beaufort County had had its first lynching," he wrote. It had not even been two weeks since the National Guard had left town.[66]

The men stood clasping pitchforks, rifles, shotguns, pistols, shovels, clubs, baseball bats, chains, and coiled ropes. Ed saw a black man down on his knees, begging. Ed couldn't hear him over the "disheveled white woman dancing around the edge of the mob, pointing at the terrified man, shouting 'That's him.'"[67]

The black man saw the sheriff. He cried out to him for help.

Contrary to habit, Ed had strapped on his .38 when he got the call. He wrote that he felt his gun growing smaller in its holster as he confronted the mob.

One man stepped out from the crowd. He told the sheriff they respected him, but they were going to take care of this one themselves. And he couldn't stop them.

Uncertainty stung at Ed's eyes like a cloud of gnats. But he had to do something. "If you think you're going to take the law into your own hands before I talk to this man, you've got trouble," he recalled saying. "You better start on me first because I'm going to cause one or two of you bad trouble before you take that man and by then, help will be here."[68]

According to McTeer, the mob relented, sort of. They insisted on following the sheriff when he went to verify the suspect's alibi. The accused claimed he had just gotten off work when the mob caught him. He said there was no way he could have been at the woman's house when the assault occurred. His boss would prove it. The moment they walked into the store where the man worked, the owner asked the suspect what he was doing back so soon. "You've only been gone a couple of hours." Ed McTeer had averted his second lynching in just over a week. But he still had a rape case to solve.[69]

McTeer, his deputies, and the rural police "began a local census" to see if there were any men suddenly missing from the area. Despite their own struggles with the sheriff, the root doctors often assisted in such situations. They provided the sheriff's office with information when it fit their interests. The root doctors did not want to see racial unrest, but they didn't seem to know anything.

McTeer often turned to Kit Singleton, a black cab driver, for good information. Singleton was ancient. He drove the McTeers into town from the train station in a buggy way back in 1904 when Jim Eddie was first elected. Everybody knew Kit and everybody talked to him, but even he came up dry this time.

The search continued through the night. Sheriff McTeer went home, leaving a deputy in charge, and returned the next morning to begin searching again. Soon, the sheriff discovered that a young man named Joe Green had suddenly left the Hardeeville area. He had been seen boarding a train shortly after the assault. The man fit the description given by the distressed woman: "short, chunky, very black, and with a heavy growth of hair on his face." McTeer learned that Green had a sister in Sumter. He found a photograph of the young man and had it broadcast to law enforcement across South Carolina and Georgia. Governor Richards offered a reward for the man's capture. Within a week, Green was in custody in Columbia. McTeer drove to the capital to question him.[70]

Green told McTeer he knew the woman and didn't rape her; he often came in her window when her husband was away. McTeer wrote that "his story was as firm as any I have heard."[71]

Still, the jury convicted Green, though on a lesser charge. He went to prison.

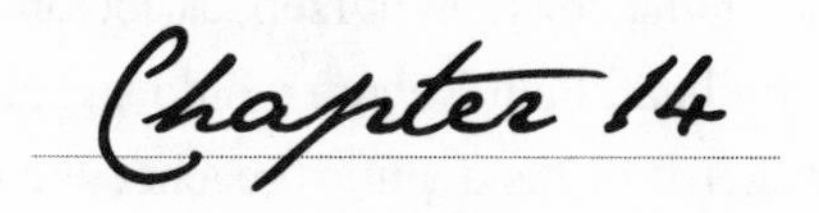

Chapter 14

The Edisto Public Works Company finished draping Beaufort with power lines at the beginning of August. For McTeer, it was hard to look at the wires strapping down the sky and not think of the life he'd lead up north. Electrical work may have been as dangerous as being sheriff, but it wasn't half as complicated. One week after the power lines were completed, the attorney of Langford's killers secured an extension for the completion of their appeals which "automatically staid an execution." The appeals process seemed interminable, but they were all locked up in Columbia where, at least for now, they would inspire neither lynching nor riot.[72]

McTeer had plenty of other things to worry about. Busting up stills had always been a big part of the sheriff's job in Beaufort County. When Ed took over from his father, he tried to be sensible about it. If he busted every still he ever heard about, he wouldn't have time to prosecute any other cases at all. If the stills were well-maintained, clean, and safe, he sometimes failed to notice them. But if somebody was using galvanized metals, the kind that could kill you or cause you to go blind, he came down hard. Often he could shut down a still without leaving the office. He'd put out word: "I hear you've got a still. I want you to take that thing down and come on in here." Sometimes the men would come in with proof that their still had been dismantled. And if you lied to him—that was when the real trouble would start.

That said, he'd been trying hard to get the moonshiners on Hilton Head ever since he came into office. The island was famous for its moonshine. That was the kind of reputation that could make the sheriff of the county look bad, if he wasn't careful. Only way there was by boat. The moonshiners all chipped in and hired a guy they called Paul Revere. It was his job to ride up and down the coast on horseback looking for sign of the sheriff. When he saw a boat, Paul Revere would signal to the moonshiners. By the time the sheriff or his deputies reached the island, everything was conspicuously clean.

Finally, Ed figured out the system. He decided to act. He went out for an inspection one day. Everything was in order. He slipped away and tied a rope across the path that Revere's horse took, then he left the island. He came back the next day with a bunch of deputies. Revere hit the rope, and crashed. McTeer and his men got the moonshiners.[73]

But that didn't slow down the overall liquor trade one bit. In 1927, federal agents started spending more time in Beaufort. They accompanied Gerald McTeer and Rural Policeman Koth on their still raids.

Ed McTeer later claimed that he caught a rural policeman running a moonshine still. With that "evidence" he pushed to reform the system and create a single law enforcement office under his own control.[74] In 1928, the County Board pushed back. County Director R.R. Legare tried to argue that McTeer should have to run again in 1928—since Jim Eddie had won his incomplete term in 1924. The County Board thought Langford's death and the crime wave could be used against the "Boy Sheriff." The Attorney General, John Daniel, wrote to Legare and told him "Mr. McTeer was elected and qualified. He is to hold for a term of four years as fixed by the Constitution. You will note," Daniel continued "that this seems an inevitable conclusion."[75]

There would be no electoral challenge, but the question of Langford's death would continue to haunt the county and its sheriff. In January 1929, Frank Francis, his father Paul Francis, and Abraham Gadsen, who had all been sentenced to death, lost what seemed to be their final appeal when the State Supreme Court upheld the lower court's decision. But there were still some questions. Justice Eugene Blease wrote a thirty-eight page opinion about the case, upholding the ruling of the previous court, but with evident distaste. He declared that "the people of South Carolina have not charged this court with dispensing either mercy or clemency." The men were scheduled to die on Friday 27 September.[76]

There was a gruesome murder the same week. A black couple saw their neighbor Elijah walking back and forth through the fields leading down to the marsh one night. They got suspicious and followed his trail. Elijah was slewfooted—one of his feet angled outwards—and they recognized his tracks, which they followed all the way down to the creek. Along the bank were long sliding tracks where something had been dragged through the thick mud. Then they saw the hands. A woman's hands stuck up from the murk, dark with gray mud and blood, as if reaching up from Hell for life itself.

The creek was several miles from town and the sheriff and Koth didn't arrive with the coroner and a doctor until the next morning. The woman's body was in bad shape by then. They carried it to a nearby schoolhouse and laid it out on a table, where Dr. Kennedy performed an examination. According to the *Gazette*, he noted that there were "several wounds" from a blunt instrument on her head and her neck was broken. The sheriff questioned the dead girl's mother, who said the deceased and her husband Elijah lived in the house with her. The couple was still asleep when she went to work at the oyster factory the previous morning. When she returned home, Elijah asked her "to tell his wife he was going to Lady's Island and would not be back until late." The next morning, the mother reported, Elijah came home and "helped her to cry, as Diane had not come home."[77]

Sheriff McTeer asked the woman if she had an axe at the house. She told him that yes, she had one, but didn't recall when she last saw it. McTeer waited at the school while Koth drove down the road to the house. There he saw blood spattered on the porch wall, though the floor looked freshly scrubbed. Koth looked closer. He could see where blood had soaked in. He pushed open the door. Blood speckled the wall and the floor inside. He found the axe under the table. Somebody had scrubbed it too, but the blood had stained the wooden handle. Koth brought it to McTeer, who arrested Elijah Smith for the murder of his wife Diane.

The story of Elijah and Diane ran in the *Gazette* below the banner headline: "Negroes Lose Appeal in Murder Case." The juxtaposition may have had some effect on the way that other case was viewed. For McTeer it was not a headline but another tragedy. He wrote that a man such as himself "suffers with the bereaved when a relative or friend is killed, and bears the shock and horror of every unspeakable act that he is forced to investigate in the course of his job."[78] He went on to write that "the images of crime that come before him are often burned into his brain forever." Ed was just twenty-five. The images and horrors were starting to pile up.

Chapter 15

The state of racial crisis seemed to be relenting. In fact, one afternoon Ed and Koth were "following a Hudson sedan on St. Helena which they suspected of hauling whiskey." When they caught up to it, they were surprised to see a white guy up front, driving, and a black guy, now frantically trying to pour the liquor out, in the back: an interracial whiskey ring.[79]

Liquor was the big news that year. The Chicago gangs had figured out the strategic value of Beaufort's countless islands, bays, coves, and harbors, which were nearly impossible to patrol. Not only that, but it was a straight shot west from Bermuda, and north from the Bahamas: You could just sail right up with tons of liquor. And there were only a few deputies and some rural policemen to patrol the intricate coastline of the county. So began in earnest the age of the high-profile rum-runners. The first sensational case came in February and the *Gazette* ran with it. "Bootleggers Hit Beaufort County In Style Pulled Off In Chicago. Hundreds of Cases of Liquor Hauled from the Swamp." The paper promised a story "spectacular in every detail, weird and even gruesome." In reality it was a rather simple smuggling story, soon overshadowed by those to come.[80]

Mr. Martin, the owner of the local oyster factory, was cutting through the swamp on some business when he came across fifteen trucks and four cars parked out in the woods. Cases of whiskey were stacked in the moonlight. Too late, he noticed the guys there with guns. One of the guys put Mr. Martin in a black car and drove him out of the swamp. They drove around for an hour or two, until the guy with the gun figured all the liquor had been loaded and the trucks were gone. He dropped Mr. Martin off in the middle of nowhere. He said goodbye and sped away.

Mr. Martin stood and watched the car disappear, then walked to the nearest phone he could find and called the sheriff.

McTeer arrested two local men seen with the truck, but he never caught the gangsters. The *Gazette* loved the sensational liquor cases, but the sheriff was focused on other things. Lucille was pregnant. He was about to have a baby to take care of. He needed to start thinking about things differently. On 1 April 1929, a daughter, Jane Lucille McTeer, was born. Ed looked at her, red-faced in her mother's arms. He saw life, time, continuity; he saw some semblance of eternity. He saw the future.

He may have been short of sleep the next day. Then again, he was always short of sleep. He didn't seem to need that much anyway. He had sheriff's blood instead. He left his wife and daughter that morning to go a meeting of the newly appointed County Board. Ed's old friends Senator Brantley Harvey and Representative Calhoun Thomas congratulated him. Then they announced some changes in the county's governance. A bill introduced by a delegate from Richland had passed, they explained to McTeer, and "the rural policeman had been abolished." Ed now had the authority to replace the rural policemen with deputies. He would also take complete responsibility for the chain-gang and the jail.[81]

McTeer later took credit for wresting control of law enforcement from the County Board. Whether or not he was responsible, he now had the "centrally controlled force under a single office" that he had long felt was essential for effective law enforcement in a county like Beaufort.[82] He held a ceremony that same day. He deputized all of the former rural policemen, including Cooler, Koth, and Randall. He also reappointed the jailor. Even those who once resented his authority seemed loyal to him now.

The South Carolina County Sheriff's Association was empowered by the changes. They met that month and elected Ed McTeer president. "The sheriff without a gun" had won.

On the Fourth of July, the *Beaufort Gazette* honored the sheriff, calling him "courteous but firm when he went to make an arrest." The *Gazette* claimed, "He has always shown the same courtesy to the rich and poor, white and black, and today has the respect of every citizen in the county."

The encomium went on to call him "a brave, fearless officer who hews the line. He is honest, sober, reliable." The *Gazette* reminded its readers that their sheriff had come home from the big city to take care of his mother and his siblings when his father died. "Later on," the paper wrote, "he married one of the finest little ladies in South Carolina and now they're the proud parents of a little daughter, but dear old mother is still with her son and daughter who is known as the youngest sheriff in the United States."

The job came with its share of glory, but the money was tight. McTeer didn't have enough to pay the interest on the farm out at Grays Hill. They lost it. He moved the family into town. He would take care of them all as he had always done. He just wasn't sure how to make it happen.

That trouble was private. The citizens probably liked having the sheriff closer to town. In the public eye, Ed was an action hero making daring liquor raids against dangerous gangsters from out of town.

Early in the morning on 7 August 1929, Deputy Cooler called McTeer. The sheriff looked at the clock. It was 3:00a.m. Cooler said he'd learned that a big shipment of liquor was coming into Bluffton that morning. McTeer and Koth met Cooler in Hardeeville. Cooler told them he was worried. He said, "They know we're watching them and they don't care."[83] The sheriff and his deputies saw two headlights coming towards them, and another set, belonging to the truck, behind it. One of the deputies got the sheriff's car in between the security car and the truck. Ed was in the passenger seat. He stuck a double barrel shotgun into the open window of the cab and hollered, "Pull over fast or you've had it." One man dove out of the passenger door and escaped into the woods, but the driver pulled the truck over. McTeer used it to block the road before the next truck came along. It stopped with the heavy screech of a swamp bird in the dark. When the gun-car slammed on the breaks, according to the *Gazette*, Ed and his men tricked "the gangsters into believing they had a large force by calling out 'Close in on the right,' 'Close in on the left,'" and generally making a lot of noise.[84] McTeer himself stepped out in front of the car. The car gunned for him. Dodging it, he fell into a barbed-wire fence. The men abandoned the car and escaped on foot. Ed got up and felt his shoes fill with blood. His leg was sliced nearly to the bone. Instead of seeking medical attention for his injury, McTeer poured whiskey on the wound, and waited with his men until light to transport the two prisoners and the liquor back to town. He was expecting an ambush.[85]

They set off at dawn. About three miles up the road, at the next sharp curve, a small army of men rushed out of the bushes, screaming, "Stop! Don't move or we'll shoot!"

McTeer hollered back, "If you do, we'll kill you! Drop your guns now!"

Agent Crowler of the Federal Prohibition Unit recognized Ed's voice. He cried out, "For God's sake don't shoot. It's Sheriff McTeer."[86]

The *Gazette* concluded the story: "After seeing all that had been captured and liquor had been destroyed, Sheriff McTeer left the situation in the hands of the federal agents. . . Sheriff McTeer then proceeded to Beaufort with two prisoners, two trucks, one automobile, one shotgun and one pistol. The investigation is however being continued."[87] Before any further investigation, however, McTeer went to the doctor to get stitches in his leg.

That was the kind of publicity a political man could use. The sheriff's office put on big displays of publicly smashing bottles. They'd set them up on the seawall back off Bay Street. Ed McTeer and Deputy Koth shot them with pistols. The bottles exploded and the liquor splashed and flowed down the wall and into the Bay; the air smelled of gunsmoke and whiskey. The AP reported that the fish got drunk. A lot of people—including the sheriff—were sad to see the liquor wasted like this. But, all was not lost. A Beaufort resident told me, "Ed McTeer was one of my grandfather Frank Webb's best friends. My grandfather owned Beaufort Hardware and they had a sort of 'club' in the rooms over the store. They supposedly had the very best liquor all during prohibition because anytime McTeer would bust a smuggler he would stash some cases of the best Scotch above the store. Many a Lowcountry bourbon drinker developed a taste for Scotch during prohibition."

A few days after the big liquor bust, Kit Singleton, the black taxi driver who acted as an informant for the sheriff, and an informal school bus driver for rural children, was hailed by four Marines. The Marines, all white men, took Singleton into the marsh and beat him. They stole his Packard and left him there in the swamp. There was widespread outrage—and not just in the black community. The *Gazette* claimed, "No negro in the South has had more white people to inquire or go to see if they could do anything to relieve his suffering than has been to see Kit Singleton." The sheriff found Singleton's car but was unable to identify his assailants.[88] He was still searching for them on 26 September, the day before the scheduled electrocution of Langford's murderers. That day, Governor Richards stayed the execution of Paul Francis, Frank Francis and Abraham Gadsen. He said "there was an element of doubt in the minds of officials and even the courts as to the guilt of murder." The Governor added that he "could not find the element of murder in this case, the officer having been shot in a clash between officers and negroes at a baseball game."[89] He cited Blease's muted appeal for clemency and mercy in the Supreme Court ruling. The big question was how three men could be guilty of one murder. After all, in the *Gazette*'s first account, Gadsen was not present at all.

Ed McTeer, his brother Gerald, Deputy Randall, and Deputy Cooler all thought of Langford. They thought about what kind of guy he was, about his wife and kids, and they knew it could be any one of them. They thought about how things were and how things had changed.

And then they fell asleep. And they woke up and they ate breakfast, and smoked cigarettes, and kept on living, and piling up those images of atrocities, and somewhere among them was Langford, murdered beside a disrupted baseball game. And an execution would not change any of it. It would always be there. Perhaps Ed was wrong when he said that he could not see the dead.

There were no riots. There was no lynching. Three men grew old in prison and died there.

Chapter 16

The Savannah River was rising on its way to the sea. The wind shoved the roiling water back. It curled over onto itself. It overflowed its banks. On 8 October 1929, "the lower section of Beaufort County was covered by water the likes of which has never been known to the memory of man since the days of the flood of Biblical fame," as the *Gazette* put it. The water "swept into the great swamp area between Ridgeland and Hardeeville, covering a section more than twenty-five miles wide, cutting off Hardeeville and neighboring villages, routing hundreds of folks from their homes, killing much game and animal life as well as devastating the section," the *Gazette* reported. Large swaths of the newly opened Coastal Highway 17 were washed away.[90]

The sheriff's phone rang late on Tuesday night. Buster Martin, a member of the County Board, told him about the disaster. By the next morning, McTeer had assembled a crew to visit the devastated area. Sheriff McTeer and his hunting and fishing buddy Clifford Baxter headed up the party that also included a physician, Senator Brantley Harvey, Representative Calhoun Thomas, and several other prominent citizens. McTeer and Baxter were "the first white men to get to the lower end of the county flooded by waters, lending first aid to the marooned folks." They got into their boat at 11:00 Wednesday morning. They scanned the country as they motored across the turbid waters, "finding negroes in trees and on houses or small islands completely surrounded by water." [91]

They rescued about seventy five people from fragile perches and dropped them off on higher ground. They returned to their launching point to pick up food, water, and other necessities supplied by the Red Cross. Many of the rescued people had been stranded for two or three days without food or water. When McTeer and Baxter reappeared, refugees rushed them in a "mad scrambling for the eats." When they had distributed all the rations, McTeer and Baxter began to use nets to fish out drowning chickens so people could cook them.[92]

The *Gazette* reported that "due to the unerring aim of the Beaufort sheriff eleven large rattle snakes and a dozen others were killed." At one point, the two men were passing beneath a low-hanging tree, the branches reflecting in the cola-colored water. The sheriff saw a rattler ready to strike his friend's head. "Beaufort's boy sheriff hit it with his rifle just in the nick of time to keep it from attacking Mr. Baxter."[93]

They came upon one black man riding on a lashed-together raft with a "keg of liquor." Though McTeer and Baxter had destroyed two stills, they did not arrest the poor fellow on the raft or confiscate his liquor—except maybe for a few swallows, to fortify their weary bones.

As darkness began to lay heavy across the submerged world, they knew they would not have time to make it back to the landing. There was still too much to do. They were on the point of collapse. The two ragged men rowed up to a submerged house. They secured the craft and climbed in the second story window. It was washed out and fetid; already dark inside. Each man found a place on the floor and wrapped himself in a Red Cross blanket and lay down. The strange gurgling of drowning animals and the distant cries of men churned the liquid darkness. In the middle of this ruined world, the two men slept.

At daylight, Ed opened his eyes. Two giant rattlesnakes were coiled on the floor at his feet. "One sported nine rattles and a button," reported the *Gazette*. McTeer moved slowly, silently. Baxter slept. McTeer put his hand on his rifle. Leaping up, he swung the rifle down, and fired twice. The gunshots echoed like ripples in water, mingling with the other eerie sounds that had taken over the world. Baxter leapt up. Stunned he looked for a human assailant, but he saw only the pieces of the serpents splattered about the floor and wall. The crisp powder from Ed's gun left a sharp tang against soft gloomy smell of decay.[94]

They climbed out the window and back into the boat. The morning sun slanted down across the dark water, reflecting the indifferent sky. The rich stench of the washed out earth was setting in. Hundreds of rats drifted by, their bodies piled up against branches in eddies. Half submerged possums looked spectral, like jelly-fish. They saw two cows sink into the muck and drown. Live animals clawed against the dark water for purchase. They screamed out zoological curses from bits of superdiluvian land. McTeer and Baxter used nets to scoop up these critters and set them down onto the floor of the boat, where they writhed and scurried. They discovered a goat on a hammock in a tree, barely able to keep its head above water. They hoisted the wet goat out of the water and aboard their craft as if it were part of some perverse rodeo. The goat began to butt at the other critters. The weird bottom of their boat scurried in the dying light. The goat pushed its way up front to cut with curved horns through the creepy air, a diabolic prow.

That day the *Gazette* reported that their rescue party came across "eight negroes in a little row boat fighting high waves in flood waters more than ten feet deep." They were going to "the flooded home of an old negro who died in their midst on a small island. They were in search of clothes to bury him in and also intended to rip from his house boards enough to fashion him a coffin." The rescuers gave them fresh water but left them alone to complete their grim task and continued to drift ten feet above the washed out ground.[95]

They spent another night in the water and finally returned late on Friday evening, three full days after venturing out into the deluged section.

Chapter 17

The last autumn of what would be remembered as the "Roaring Twenties" had slipped inside the air and the trees and made them stand sharp, attentive and crisp, like soldiers in freshly pressed uniforms.

The Thursday before Thanksgiving: the night rose up in a fog from the earth and dripped down from the heavens like thick wet paint. Gerald McTeer was driving down the highway on his way home. He had always been a big man, but now his girth flowed over the sides of the seat and pushed the car's chassis downward to the sandy road, so that it rolled with a comic, lopsided gait, like a limping man. He was still drinking a lot, even as he busted stills and smugglers. His headlights knocked narrow dents into the dark night. In the yellow light he saw a car in a ditch just outside the town of Burton. A man was standing behind the car, looking down at it. The *Gazette* reported that "Gerald McTeer, brother of the sheriff," pulled over to assist. But when the driver began to "curse and rave at the ones who had stopped to help him. . . Mr. McTeer called his brother and told him to come and get the man." Gerald did not act in the capacity of deputy that night but awaited the arrival of Ed and Deputy Koth. They arrived with Mr. Oltmann, Ed's and Gerald's brother-in-law, who was visiting from Charelston.[96]

It is not clear what Gerald did that night, but I can conjure an image of him waddling away through the dark, lurching a bit just before he squeezed himself into the old car, slamming the door and swerving down the road. He was like Sir John Flastaff, unrenounced, incorporated into Henry's regime, legitimate, but not entirely reliable.

At any rate, Gerald was gone before his brother arrested the driver of the ditched car, a Marine named Leslie Fisk, who was still raving when they got there and would not calm down.

McTeer cuffed Fisk, and sat him in the front seat beside Koth, who drove. Ed stooped down to crawl into the back seat beside his brother-in-law, Mr. Oltmann. "You'll regret arresting me," said Fisk. "I have a notion to step on the starter and tear the engine up."[97]

The car pushed its way up the road a few miles. They saw the lights of another car approaching. Fisk reached over and grabbed the wheel. He screamed he would send them all to hell. He threw his weight toward Koth and tried to send the car into the oncoming traffic. Ed reached up around the seat to grab Fisk as the car careened and squealed. Koth fought for the wheel. He rocked the car back and forth. Ed began to pound Fisk's head with his fists. They could hear children scream as their faces were washed out by the approaching lights. The cars were about to collide. Koth gained control of the car and swerved away from the passing family, crashing into the opposite ditch.

After they pulled the sheriff's car from the ditch, they took Fisk to a doctor, then locked him up in the jail where he would await trial. The *Gazette's* editor, E.O. Wilson, approvingly commented on the "Boy Sheriff's" remarkable courage and Deputy Koth's presence of mind.[98] McTeer noted that "in all of the experiences with various types of criminals, this man was the worst."[99]

Chapter 18

Perhaps it was ironic that Black Thursday's stock market crash was not hurting the black people of the Sea Islands as 1929 ended. The construction of the Lady's Island Bridge in 1927 had opened new opportunities for the Gullah. They had abundant waters and fertile soil. They had oysters, fish, shrimp, and produce. Everyone had a garden with tomatoes, potatoes, peas, and corn. Now they could sell to the outside world. Truck farming was the new economy on the sea islands.

In 1930, The *Gazette* published an editorial called "When Negro Life is Easiest." E.O. Wilson, the paper's editor, noted that "St. Helena Island, with its four thousand five hundred blacks and less than one hundred whites is the first township to pay the yearly taxes. . . and not one single one of the eight hundred or more of the little self-owned island homes have they ever foreclosed on a mortgage." The editorial noted that "considering the supreme struggle of poverty in the today with its unemployment and high living costs and all of which strike at the negro first, this record truly on St. Helena stands out as being unique."

Samuel Hopkins Adams, writing for *True*, remarked "Prosperous Negroes are not uncommon in the Lowcountry of South Carolina; Beaufort's crab factory, its oyster factory and vast truck gardens surrounding it pay good wages by local standards." Adams was especially impressed by "the costly character of the household equipment and the impressive appearance of the car into which it was being loaded," when he first saw Dr. Buzzard, probably the wealthiest man on the island. When the Baptist church burned down, Dr. Buzzard bankrolled a new one.[100]

Ed knew he could still learn from root doctors like Dr. Buzzard who garnered so much authority from a simple belief. "Most of the elders who knew McTeer personally will tell you that he did listen to Mr. Robinson initially," Marquetta Goodwine—who calls herself Queen Quet of the Gullah Geechee Nation—wrote in an email. "He also did not come on the island and harass people, which was very common with Anglo sheriffs in the South toward people of African descent. He was a pleasant man to the community and did not try to criminalize everyone as some others do even today. His relationship with Mr. Robinson was one that showed that he did respect the 'gift' and the role of Mr. Robinson as a representative of our people and as a leader of St. Helena Island."

Goodwine called Dr. Buzzard a leader of St. Helena but his influence went beyond the island. Like McTeer, he was a representative. A big part of both of their jobs depended on public opinion. The magic of the sheriff's badge was a matter of life and death. The scene of every crime was drawn out in proximity to the power of his badge.

Ed saw this all too clearly that January when a white man named Joe Rivers cut and killed Alex Washington, a black man, over seventy-five cents in a dice game. "Feeling was running high against Rivers," the *Gazette* reported, and "a large number of both white and colored people" had spent a cold and rainy night searching for him in the woods and swamps.[101]

Joe Rivers, the killer, slipped out of the woods at Stuart Point. He found a black man named Joe Washington standing in the rain with a shotgun, waiting for him. Joe Washington was not related to Alex but the two knew one another. Washington told Rivers to halt. The white man turned and ran. Washington aimed and fired, shooting Rivers in the leg. Rivers cried out and fell. Washington apprehended the wounded man. He got a friend to help load Rivers into the car. Joe Washington gunned it towards town; he didn't like having the wounded white killer in his car and he couldn't get to the sheriff's fast enough.

The paper reported that "after arriving at the sheriff's house a large crowd of colored people gathered around the car, but Washington stood guard with his gun drawn and warned them not to touch Rivers: and that no one could put their hands on him but the sheriff."[102]

McTeer came out and took charge of Rivers. In his pockets, the sheriff found forty cents and some dice. He drove the prisoner towards the jail. On the way there, Rivers admitted that he had killed Alex Washington, but he denied robbing him. He stabbed him with a knife, which he lost as he ran through the woods that night.

The sheriff pulled up at the jailhouse. His headlights reflected off the bumpers of cars that filled the lot. There were wagons over to the side. A big crowd, mostly black, surged up around them in the dark with flashes of angry and bitter-pinched faces and teeth set towards vengeance. It was the same kind of crowd that the sheriff had encountered in Hardeeville two years earlier, only these faces were of another color. "The sheriff notified them that no one could see Rivers; that he was in his charge and he would protect him. The crowd then dispersed," read the next issue of the *Gazette*.[103]

If that wasn't magic . . . .

Chapter 19

No one had filed to run against him by spring of 1930 and it didn't seem like anyone would. That was good, because Lucille was pregnant again and Jane was just barely a year old. A potential candidate quipped that Ed timed it so that he had his children on election years.

He made several more high profile liquor busts that discouraged any late-blooming opponents from rising up. Who could run against a man who came across like a superhero in the paper every week? Even when there weren't floods or chases or shoot-outs, Ed McTeer seemed too lucky for a realistic opponent to challenge.

Ed got a call one day from Mr. Brown, the jailor, who told him a trustee had seen some suspicious things going on in the main cell where eight prisoners were currently being held. The sheriff drove down to the jailhouse and discovered one of the bars on the door sawed almost in half. Buried in the ashes of a wood stove, McTeer found the saw. He suspected an inmate named John because the man's wife had just brought him some clothes. The *Gazette* reported that John was considered a "desperate character," because he tried to pull a gun on his arresting officer. The sheriff made sure that he was "placed where it was impossible for him to try and make another getaway." Mr. Brown wasted no time making sure that "new locks and double bars were at once placed on the doors."[104]

Any time of night or day something like that could happen and Ed would be blamed. If the prisoners had busted out and anything bad had come of it, half the white men in the county would have signed up to run against the sheriff. Unemployment was over thirty-seven percent statewide. Plenty of people were out in the malarial swamp just waiting for the moment to take down the sheriff for the sake of a steady pay-check.

Because of the trustee, Ed got credit for foiling the getaway plan. He also collected political capital to get the improvements he wanted for the jail.

McTeer was so lucky that some people figured the sheriff was charmed. His African collections had people calling him a root doctor. They were joking, of course. But it was a serious matter. It was not uncommon that he'd get a call where someone out on St. Helena had burnt down her shack because she believed that some root doctor had cast a spell on it. Or some man had killed himself because the root doctor had made him impotent. Using roots was not illegal (giving out ointments or potions was), but it was still harmful. He began to think of other ways to combat it. He began talking to doctors around Beaufort. They'd all had patients complain they'd been rooted. They came to the doctors desperate, these people, and the doctors would tell them that it was all in their minds. That stuff isn't real. Don't let it worry you. Then it would get worse, and the patient would stop eating or drinking and would sometimes die. "Undetermined natural causes" was the coroner's code.

Chapter 20

Ed got a tip on a big stash of liquor in Pocotaglio. He took Gerald and Koth and a magistrate named Mr. Lott with him to investigate one April night. They walked through a graveyard by Stony Creek, casting four shadows. It was dark and the branches of the live oaks hung low and heavy over the graves as they approached the woods at the edge of the graveyard. The four men paused, scanning the terrain. "Jump!" Mr. Lott screamed to the sheriff. Ed jumped and while he was in the air, Lott shot the reptile the sheriff had been standing on: a six-foot rattle snake. The *Gazette* reported "that our sheriff is as brave as any man who ever put on a badge but from what we can learn the perspiration was running into his shoes when he realized how near he came to being 'knocked out' by a snake with eight rattles and a button." Ed was still shaken when he discovered the hundred and seventy sacks of bonded booze they'd been looking for. A random sampling on sight revealed a real haul: bourbon, rum, even champagne.[105]

McTeer had to worry about a lot more than snakes: He knew the smugglers and rumrunners kept an eye on him. Often, when he knew he was being watched, he came home at night and ate dinner with Lucille and baby Jane. Then he went upstairs, stood in front of the window and undressed. He turned off the lights and lay down. Fifteen minutes later, he got up and got dressed in the dark. He slipped out back and went over to the jail. He slid into the waiting black car, an emblem of the state painted on the door. He had his own informers and eyes all over the county. They called him directly when they saw something suspicious.

One Sunday in the fall of 1930, Ed got a call. He and his deputies chased a big liquor boat near Bluffton, but they lost it because their small craft couldn't keep up. McTeer had the county on high alert. He got a tip the next day. There was a big boat anchored out near the Whale Branch. In a sworn statement, McTeer said he brought Gerald, Koth, Randall, and two other deputies with him. He told the court that "upon reaching the landing we noticed several cars with out-of-state licenses. One white man was seen to run from the landing towards the woods. We took possession of a rowboat with an outboard motor" and set out for the ship. McTeer recalled that "the wind was picking up and the swells and chop were mounting ever higher."[106] Koth knelt in the bow of the boat. The other deputies used buckets to bail water over the sides. As the craft reached the middle of the river the swells rocked the boat. The waves shattered against Koth's chest. When they finally managed to pull up alongside the ship, its captain cried out into the yelping winds and sloshing sea: "Don't come any closer! Identify yourselves." McTeer replied in Gullah "making my words unintelligible, edging ever closer to the boat every second."[107]

The "captain ran from the stern into the cabin where he secured an automatic shotgun." McTeer would later write that when he got aboard, he hit the captain over the back of the head with his pistol.[108] But in his sworn statement, McTeer said, "I jumped up on the deck and told him to drop it, which he did." The sheriff got the gun. The deputies came aboard. They had the crew covered, a group of blacks from Nassau, the ship's homeport.

The ship was loaded with thousands of bottles of bonded liquor. As the sheriff questioned the men, a weird story emerged. The captain was a black Bahamian named Octavis Russell who testified that, although he was the boat's captain, there was a white man named Mr. Rawlins in charge of the liquor. When they got to South Carolina, Mr. Rawlins went ashore. "While he was gone," Russell testified, "a white man come along in a row boat and asked me what I was loaded with, and he come aboard and saw the liquor and ask me who the liquor belong to and I told him the owner was ashore, then he asked me whether I wanted him to carry me in or let him get as much liquor as he wanted, and I told him to do what he wanted to do and he took some liquor and left." Other crewmembers told the *Gazette* that it was three men who came aboard and that they had claimed to be the law.[109]

Shortly after the bust, the sheriff got a call that offered some unsavory answers to the questions this story raised. A policeman named Harry Boyle resigned from his position. (The *Gazette* would contemptuously call him a man "temporarily serving on the police force for a few days.") In the course of his resignation, he told his superior that he had heard that Deputy Koth had gone aboard and robbed the liquor boat before it was captured.[110]

Koth heard about the allegation. He filed a complaint against Boyle, charging him with libel and slander. The Sheriff's department handcuffed Boyle, and locked him up. Boyle got a lawyer who told Judge Lotte that the case should be dismissed. Judge Lotte decided against Boyle and set his bail at $700—far more than the bond of the smugglers themselves. Several days later the *Gazette* mocked Boyle: "Up to present time he has not furnished same."

In court the following week, Boyle read an apology to Koth, which he had written in jail. The *Gazette* printed it in its entirety: "When I sent my resignation to the mayor through my immediate supervisor I felt that it was due to him and myself to give my reasons. This I did in the strict confidence of an official communication made in the line of duty," he said. "I assumed no responsibility for the truth of the information report nor did I suppose the confidential report would be made public. It is regrettable that it was and I am very sorry indeed. Nothing could be further from my intention in making my report." But, he warned, "if you as a police officer cannot report to your superior officer information coming to you without being criminally prosecuted you would be seriously handicapped in the performance of your duty." He added that his time in jail had convinced him that the information he had offered had been false.[111]

The Beaufort *Gazette* never published another word about the white robber and there is no record of further investigation into the allegations.

A short time later, Deputy Koth raided a still in the woods. When he got there he found himself face to face with former Sheriff Bailey, his big pale face staring mean through the dark. Koth had to take the former sheriff, defeated by Jim Eddie McTeer back in 1924, to jail. He charged the former sheriff with manufacturing and possessing contraband liquor. Judge Lotte set Bailey's bond at three hundred dollars.

Around the same time Bailey was busted, McTeer's friend Arthur Paul piloted the sheriff's crew for another big liquor haul. Paul had a good boat and knew the waters as well as anyone.

Arthur Paul is no longer alive but his two sons, Arthur Junior and Emmett, are. I went out to Pleasant Point Plantation on Lady's Island to see if they knew anything about the old Prohibition liquor busts. Arthur Junior, the older brother, is a large, respectable-looking man with short white hair. He was wearing a polo shirt and standing in the garage when I arrived. Emmett, the younger brother, had long thin hair and a more wrinkled face. He was wearing shorts and flip-flops. Arthur Junior sat in a chair; Emmett flopped back on the couch. Emmett was the boat co-ordinator for the movie *Forrest Gump,* which was filmed in and around Beaufort. When they got around to talking about liquor, Arthur Junior said: "Papa had a boat and a motor and that was something the sheriff's department didn't have and he was asked to go with Ed and also just to drive him up to where he had to be and unfortunately it was to arrest people sometimes. He went with him that way in Broad River one time. They confiscated a lot of whiskey," he said. "He ever tell you about that?" he asked his brother.

"I heard him talking about things like that," Emmett replied.

"He went on that particular case when we lived in Salt Creek, which was right below Parris Island. I was only two probably then and I don't remember it that much but they talked about it a good many times years later. What they did was they put in the river there and went down the Broad River until Ed told papa to cut the motor off. They didn't want to make any noise and he saw the silhouette of a barge and they pulled right up to it and Ed got out and said 'you just stay here and let me go inside' and he went inside and he came back out and he had two people, boys, in handcuffs and then they uh, Hubert Randall was the deputy wasn't he?"

“Michael. I don’t know,” Emmett replied.

“No. No, Deputy Michael’s much later.”

“You’re a lot older than me,” Emmett yawned.

“They pulled up in a pick-up truck and Ed put the boys in handcuffs in the car and put them inside and went to see what was in the barge and bonded whiskey was the whole thing. What they did before they left, they just went and randomly picked out booze, cases and put in that truck up as high as it would go. Ed and Papa left and came on back to where he lived in Salt Creek—Albergotti. Papa said Ed—not Ed but one of the deputies—parked the truck in his yard, took the two boys to jail in his car, and Ed said, ‘Now look, we’ll come by here to get the pickup truck in the morning and naturally if anything is missing from it we can’t hold you responsible for it.’ Dad said: ‘Sure.’ Said it took him all night to unload the truck.”

Chapter 21

Lucille gave birth to Georgiana McTeer on 29 December 1930. They named her after Ed's sister. They had two girls now and both were healthy. He had been sheriff for five years by 1931. He had been tested by two elections, and had not yet turned thirty. He was training Zeke, his youngest brother, to join the department when he finished school the next year. Gerald was already on the force, but things weren't going so well there and Ed knew he would have to deal with it.

Still, all the children loved big old Gerald. He had a parking space on Bay Street and no one else would dare take it. He would pull up there on a Saturday morning, find the first kid and send him to get a "co-cola." Then he'd sit there in the car all morning giving out candy and talking. He was more visible than Ed in that way and one of those children—now a retired man—told me, "Ed was just doing real estate even way back then. It seemed like Gerald ran the department."

Zeke had been a twelve year-old boy when their father died. Ed had practically raised him, letting him ride along on calls, and now he was going to be a full-fledged deputy. Zeke was just out of high school but they'd accused Ed of "hiring young deputies" five years ago and he'd won that election just fine. Soon after taking office, Walter started busting stills. On one raid, he found a concealed weapon on a black preacher on Hilton Head. He handcuffed the man. Members of his flock walked by. The preacher tried to hide his head. Walter greeted the passers-by warmly. It was his first arrest.

Their sister Maddie worked the switchboard, so she was first with the news that the Pittsburgh police department had caught Willie Heyward, one of the two brothers who had shot officer Carden back in 1925, just before Ed's father took office. Randall, who was still a deputy, had picked up Carden and carried him to the car under fire. Now, seven years later, he would finally come face to face with the man who had tried to kill him. When the sheriff and Deputy Randall got to Pittsburgh, Heyward did not recognize them.

Heyward told them how he and his brother escaped. "We went into the woods and that night got a boat and went up the river to Seaboard trestle where we done away with our guns. From there we went to Allendale and caught a train and kept on riding until we got to Philadelphia and have been working there ever since," under assumed names. The *Gazette* wrote a confusing account of the confession: "Ben shot Mr. Carden using his name; that he fired running across a field, but later changed his mind; he said Ben was the one who had slipped up in the bushes and tried to kill Mr. Randall while he was carrying the body of Mr. Carden." The *Gazette* also gave Sheriff McTeer credit for apprehending the criminal, claiming that when he took office, he "began a search for the two Heyward boys and the result was that he located Willie in Pittsburgh where he had him arrested and he is safely in the penitentiary in Columbia, S.C. where he was carried Sunday night by the officers who brought him back."[112]

Heyward hired two Savannah lawyers who claimed that their client could not get a fair trial in Beaufort. As evidence, they cited the sheriff's manifest fear that trouble would break out if he brought the prisoner to the county where the crime occurred. McTeer addressed this directly: "I never once thought of any trouble when I brought Heyward here: my reason for leaving him in the penitentiary was on account of the condition of the Beaufort jail." Might as well make another push for a new jail. "I think it's an unjust statement of these gentlemen to make: leaving the impression that people had intended to start trouble in case he was brought here. As far as feelings being high, that is something I have never heard since I returned with Heyward."[113]

Ed had come a bit closer to evening the score. The past could not be altered. But it could be remembered and respected. Arresting Heyward,

McTeer was still putting his father's estate in order, providing human continuity in the midst of an inhuman world. That was justice.

Now that Zeke was on the force, there was a greater sense of continuity. It was good for Ed to have someone to train. The other deputies either predated him in service, like Randall and Cooler, or were older, like Gerald. Each was connected to a world without Ed. And perhaps in some way or another, each still bristled against his authority.

Nobody bristled like Ed's old friend Mattie Simmons. Mattie was the best outdoorsman Ed knew. He'd gotten a job as a prohibition officer in Florida. "The bootleggers had been getting bold," Ed explained. They'd been shooting at the officers and the agency was looking for men "not to be trifled with." Mattie Simmons had this reputation and, according to McTeer, he got the job done. "He did such a thorough job that the prohibition administrator thought he had better release him before the score got too high. So he came back home." If the prohibition forces wouldn't have him, Mattie knew where his talents would be appreciated. Ed heard Mattie was on the wrong side of the liquor game. One night, Ed and his deputies were making a liquor bust. There was a stand-off; guns out on all sides. One of the criminals said, "Don't shoot, that's Sheriff McTeer" in a voice that Ed recognized as Mattie's. The bootleggers suddenly scrambled away through the dark woods.[114]

McTeer later wrote that Simmons "was a man born in the wrong era. A man who could have made his way to the top of many professions, but Mattie could not survive if adventure and danger were not around the bend."[115] Like McTeer, Mattie Simmons had sheriff's blood. Ed must have thought himself lucky: He got adventure and danger within the confines of the law. He was the law and so half his life had to be outside of it. He saw every aspect of the world, good and evil. He collected stories and eventually began to think that "I'd heard all the tales of woe and seen all the unusual sights that could possibly be seen."[116]

Of course, he hadn't seen the nudist colony that was opening up on Cat Island. . . not yet. But he'd sure as hell heard enough about the place. A couple named Gilbert and Gertrude Parks, of New York, had bought the four hundred acre island a while back. In the spring of 1932 they were ready to come down with about ten other couples to start their utopian commune. Mr. Parks said, "Like Thoreau we can try to escape from the doubtful values of civilization," and recreate a society along the lines of Plato's *Republic*. He said that they had purchased the island—adjacent to Parris Island because "any attempt on the part of a group of people to start a utopian society would need the isolation of an island for success."[117]

It was looking like an island might not be enough. The *State* newspaper in Columbia had created an uproar with a story about the group's naturalist philosophy. The prudish Governor Ibra Blackwood said if they did not begin to dress decently he would "order the sheriff of Beaufort County to arrest them." McTeer thought of how to respond. He knew he was a constable of the governor and would have to follow any orders he was given. But he did not believe the governor was right. When asked, he told the *Gazette*: "If I want to take my clothes off in my bathroom it's my business. If anyone else comes into my bathroom, I can prosecute them." He was even more pointed when talking to the *Savannah Morning News*. He told them, "There's such a thing as personal liberty in this country. If the governor wants to go nude about the governor's mansion whose business would it be but his own as long as he did it in private?"[118]

Just wait, he and the deputies laughed, the chiggers, noseeums, poison ivy, and mosquitoes would discourage nudity far more effectively than law enforcement. From all reports, though, and there were a lot of them, the nudists knew what they were doing. They had built homes and were preparing gardens. By the next year they had thirty-five people living there and Mr. Parks claimed: "Our planned economy is busy putting up over 700 quarts of fruits and vegetables so that from now on our only food purchases need be coffee, tea, sugar, and condiments. At present, our garden supplies fifteen different vegetables. The average meal offers a variety of at least eight of these. Plums and blackberries are now put away as jam and jelly for the winter. Our pear and melon crops will be abundant. The woods are filled with wild grapes. Figs will about double last year's yield."[119]

Eventually, some papers had to be served and it fell to the sheriff to go out there and serve them. His wife, Lucille, reminded him that he did not personally serve papers anymore. She recommended that he send someone else out to the island. Well, he figured, might as well give it to young Zeke, barely eighteen years old. Ed warned Zeke about the "pitfalls he would encounter" and reminded him that they would be waiting for him to return with the papers. Zeke did not come back for four days. It looked like it could become a scandal. Before too many people found out, Ed sent his oldest deputy to retrieve his youngest. "He found Zeke living like a king. As an emissary from the sheriff's office he'd been received with open arms," Ed wrote. "I could tell from the look on his face it wouldn't do to give him a tongue lashing. All I could think," McTeer recalled, "was 'there but for the grace of God go I.'"[120]

Chapter 22

Zeke and the nudists seemed to be about the only ones living like kings. Even the truck farmers on St. Helena were hurting now. Just two years earlier the *Gazette* had reported that the island had no foreclosures and was always first to pay its taxes. Now, a grand jury was investigating the sheriff for being "too lax in the collection of back taxes." The grand jury reported: "After investigating we wish to commend the sheriff on his very efficient and humane method of collecting these taxes." A Georgia paper reported on the story under the title "A Merciful Sheriff" and claimed that McTeer was "making haste slowly in the collection of taxes because he does not care to foreclose upon those who through stress of hard times and circumstances have not been able to meet their obligations to the state and county."[121] He still remembered what it had been like for his family to lose their farm.

Still, sometimes he couldn't help but foreclose. Sheriff's sales—tax auctions—became an increasingly important part of his job. He would hold an auction and sell off the property in order to pay back taxes. He held several auctions a month and it threatened to keep getting worse.

It was more often now that he got calls from Will Keyserling, who managed the community welfare funds. "Keyserling calling, Sheriff. Do you know Mose Drayton or Perry Claire?"[122]

"Yes, Mr. Keyserling," McTeer would answer. "He has been sick and has no one to help him. Please do what you can."[123] There were breadlines and food warehouses. Chief Scott, of the Beaufort Police Department, caught one guy named Perkins Williams stealing chickens. Evidence on his person lead Scott to believe he'd been involved in a store robbery. Chief Scott told the sheriff, who took Deputy Koth with him to investigate Williams' known associates on St. Helena. They visited the home of a man named Sammie Major. As they searched Major's house, they discovered something strange: "A case of roast beef."

They arrested Major and took him in for questioning. He told them he'd gotten the roast beef from Perkins Williams. That was good news, if it was true, since Scott had Williams in jail on the chicken charge. While he was on the island, the sheriff went by Leslie Armstrong's house. There, they found "half a case of meat, half a case of beef." Armstrong, too, said that he'd gotten the goods from Williams.[124]

Back in Beaufort, the sheriff went to Williams and told him that both Major and Armstrong said they got the meat from him. "Well, Sheriff," Perkins said. "If they have told you that, I will tell all. . . Yes, we stole the meat from the Beaufort County Emergency Relief Warehouse. Both of them fellows were with me."[125]

The meat was unmarked. They drove out to the warehouse. It was clear it had been broken into. But no one had noticed that the warehouse had been burgled until Perkins told McTeer. R.R. Legare, the former Chair of the County Board who had tried to finagle McTeer out of office in 1928, was the program's administrator. When they told him that the warehouse was robbed, he couldn't say how much food had been stolen. A couple of days later, U.S. Marshals came and arrested the beef burglars and held them until they were tried in a Federal Court.[126]

It wasn't just stealing. Random, violent crime was on the rise. It was not uncommon for the sheriff to have to secure an insane man or woman. One night, he went out on a call. He shone his flashlight on a madman in baggy pants stabbing a house with a pitchfork. He was mumbling and yelling. Koth slipped around the corner. The man looked at McTeer, then charged him with the pitchfork. McTeer shot him in the leg, but the man didn't stop. McTeer shot again. Still the madman kept coming. McTeer thought he would have to kill him. McTeer shot again. Finally, Koth tackled the man. "When we got him to jail," McTeer wrote, "I saw in the light that his trouser legs were quite full and my bullets had passed right through them without ever touching him."[127]

Right after that the sheriff had to secure two thrashing mad men on opposite sides of the county on the same day. He asked a witness "what was wrong with their people going crazy?"

Someone answered: "The Depression is got us."[128]

Insane eyes cast a man like Ed McTeer in a larger frame. Craziness increased his power. Often he did not even have to use it. One night, McTeer recognized a thief by his tracks and traced him down. Somebody heard him singing the Jimmy Rogers song "He's in the Jailhouse Now," as he escorted the man to his cell; it was always one of his favorites.[129] Sometimes he sat on the porch with his little girls and played his old Martin guitar and sang it for them. With the way of things, Lucille was pregnant again, swelling with the summer and the sound of the crickets and cicadas.

Ed was running against B.B. Paul that year. Captain Vecchio hosted the stump meeting at his dock. It was hardly a race at all. McTeer beat Paul 1,551 votes to 236. Three days later, Lucille gave birth to Sally, the couple's third daughter.

Ed was again looking to the future. Many of the once-rich northern industrialists were taking hits on the stock market and finding themselves forced to sell their hunting preserves down south. Ed knew many of these men. He had hunted with them. He knew other men in Beaufort with whom he could pool together money in order to buy the preserves. If they could kick this Depression, people would want to move down here, just like the nudists, where the living was good.

The nudist thing was still a controversy. The governor sent two constables down to Beaufort and ordered Ed to take them to Cat Island. According to McTeer, the two constables brought their wives. "I told them what we were liable to encounter, and did all I could to get them to leave their wives in town to tour the old churches while we were gone." The constables insisted that their wives could wait in the boat while the men went ashore. "As we approached," wrote McTeer, "the island lookout must have spotted us and thought Zeke was returning, for as we disembarked at the wharf a flock of naked men and women came flying down the path towards us, squealing 'aloha' and other things."

According to McTeer one of the constables shouted "Let's get the hell out of here!" McTeer overheard one of the wives say, "Well, I never!"

He responded, "Neither have I, Madam."[130]

The *State* ran the story: "Constables Flee at Sight of Nudists."

Chapter 23

"The Depression is got us." People were desperate for something to save them. The answers were often spiritual. WPA narratives from the Lowcountry in the 1930s detail the cult of Father Divine, a charismatic Harlem preacher who claimed he was God. Like the Nudists, he created communes that produced vegetables, which he sold all around the country. A.J. Liebling and St. Clair McKelway began their 1936 profile of him: "Father Divine has said on more than one occasion that he is God. . . The effect of this bold claim on the press and the government of the city in which he makes his headquarters has been remarkable. The papers, on the whole, have appeared to regard his works as miraculous. The city government has been singularly deferential towards him."[131] His followers, a relatively law-abiding bunch, really believed he was God. McTeer was not quite so deferential, but he understood that during hard times people were seeking transcendence.

The root doctors had the ability to help people; instead they were making it worse. Whenever McTeer thought he could prove that Buzzard had distributed a potion or powder, the witness would suddenly refuse to testify. Kit Singleton drove the taxi from town out to Doctor Buzzard's place on St. Helena. He would wait there for the customers, who were excited when they came back to the cab, telling Kit everything Dr. Buzzard had said or done or given them. Kit would tell McTeer. Then Buzzard got word of this, and told his clients the spell wouldn't work—or that it would kill them—if they spoke of it. Soon Singleton returned to town each night in silence.

Whatever Dr. Buzzard was doing, it was making him rich. Sam McGowan, the postmaster of St. Helena Island, told the sheriff that Mr. Robinson had thousands of dollars in money orders that he'd received over time in his P.O. Box. He'd recently come to cash them, wearing his dark glasses and his sharp suit. Mr. McGowan asked Dr. Buzzard to sign the money orders, then he'd be happy to cash them. *Sign them?* Not Stephaney Robinson. He ripped them all up into little pieces that he let rain down into the trash.

McTeer told a story about a man who wanted to sue his ex-wife. The man told the lawyer that the woman put a hex on him when he left her for another woman. When he came back to get some stuff, she took his underwear, sprinkled it with powder, and burned it. She told him, "You have been good in bed but from now on you will never be able to be with any woman and satisfy her. Now go."[132]

It had been a year, now, and he hadn't performed "his duty as a husband, not even once."[133] The lawyer told the man that there was no legal recourse. Then the lawyer told him it was all in his mind. Three weeks later, the man killed himself.

Maybe it was time for the sheriff to deal with these root doctors. McTeer knew that witchcraft could help people. Instead, the root doctors went for the money. They gave potions. They put hexes on people. If he couldn't stop the root doctors, maybe he could counteract them. If they were poison, he would be the antidote.

McTeer started talking to the medical doctors in town again. The county was full of people who felt like they had been cursed. McTeer asked the doctors if they thought research into root work would be medically valuable. They all agreed: "There was a need for someone who had the power to take spells off. They frankly admitted that their training had not qualified them for this procedure," McTeer reported, "and urged me to continue my research."[134]

Ed McTeer had reached a second turning point in his life. He reflected on his thinking for a newspaper reporter: "I said, 'How can a doctor lower himself to the level of someone who has a hex on him? I chose myself as a messiah to do this.'"[135]

Chapter 24

"Fate and the environment in which I lived did not leave me much choice in choosing which form of the occult practices I would follow: African Witchcraft."[136] A messiah must first of all believe in himself. McTeer wrote: "You must have the power to make yourself believed, but even more important, you must believe in yourself."[137] McTeer clearly possessed this prerequisite and began to let it be known that he had the power to take roots off people. At first, he worked with other doctors in order to develop some swamp cred.

In one of his earliest cases, a prominent white farmer came to the sheriff's office and asked him to lock up the root doctor who'd hexed one of the young black women who lived on his farm. The farmer described the situation to Ed. She had a stretch of bad luck. She began to think of possible enemies. Suddenly, all the disconnected misfortunes seemed to fall into place, to make sense, to fit into an order: she'd been rooted. It got worse. She was unable to work, eat or sleep. She was wasting away in bed, staring blankly up at the ceiling. The white man repeated that he would like to bring charges against the root doctor.

"We don't know for sure if there's been a root doctor involved," McTeer counseled. He asked the farmer to drive him out to the woman's house. When they got there, McTeer put on his dark glasses. Inside the cabin, McTeer saw the "emaciated middle aged woman," lying in bed, unable to move. McTeer turned to the white farmer. "Someone has put a strong root on this woman, Hal," he said. "I can feel it all around me . . . someone has put a strong root on this woman." He said that he could save her, but only if the farmer was willing to pay a hefty fee. McTeer said that in order to impress the serious nature of the situation onto the mind of the woman; he would not actually take any money. McTeer told them it was such a strong spell that he would have to bring in Dr. Hawk to help. McTeer later explained: "The reason I'd chosen Dr. Hawk was that the woman believed her root had been put on by Dr. Buzzard and I didn't want to leave the avian world and confuse her. Besides, a hawk sounded quite fierce compared to a buzzard and I thought it might help."

McTeer was starting to master the poetics of root. Dr. Hawk was "an imposing man, about 6'2" and weighing 250." When he was not off working in graveyards, Dr. Hawk was a greengrocer. His store had been robbed and McTeer had recovered the stolen money; he owed the sheriff a favor. Dr. Hawk agreed to help when the sheriff showed up at his place that night. They drove through the darkness to the house and snuck into the yard. They stayed a short while. Then McTeer dropped Dr. Hawk back home.[138]

The next day the two men returned to the house. The woman waited on a cot that had been pulled out onto the porch. Friends and family stood around her, curious and terrified. McTeer stepped first from his sheriff's car. He looked out at the crowd and told them Dr. Hawk "stayed up all night in the graveyard talking with spirits and he tells me he is ready to save this woman."[139]

When he announced the doctor, he pronounced his name forcefully, letting it fly from his mouth like a bird from the arm of the falconer: "Dr. Hawk!"

Dr. Hawk leapt from the car. He ordered them to stay back. He said they would die if they got too close. He stomped around the yard. He muttered in the unknown tongue. The sounds rolled from his mouth with the rhythm of percussive music. He cut a branch from a peach tree by the side of the house. He bent the branch back on itself and used it as a divining rod. He waved it around. He staggered through the yard. He kicked up dust. He finally let go of the stick, flinging it. It pointed like a quivering arrow at the root McTeer and Dr. Hawk had planted in the yard together the previous night. Dr. Hawk held it aloft and declared it a death root. He destroyed it. The woman was healed.

Afterwards, McTeer wrote: "I don't know how much the demonstration helped Dr. Hawk's business but it firmly established me as a mover among the root doctors and indeed as a root doctor myself."[140]

Chapter 25

The magic was working. In 1938 Ed managed to buy "one of Beaufort's old homes . . . one of the most beautiful sites on the Bay." It had been owned by "the late Maude Odell, Beaufort's noted actress of many years who died in New York about a year ago."[141] The place was grand. It was a perfect home for the sheriff and his family. He even had a room for his mother. It was barely a block to the courthouse and not much farther from the jail. He envisaged building his own museum in the big back yard. He had helped start the Beaufort Museum when he found an old Civil War cannon in the Bay, but he wanted a place where he could keep his growing collection of weapons, artifacts and oddities, which now included some of the "bad roots" he took off people.

The big white house acted like a huge root on the white citizens in the small town of Beaufort itself. It was symbolic. As the shrieval home, it protected the man who protected them. It gave the citizenry some comfort to know where the sheriff lived, to know where they could go late of a night when things had gone wrong. They drove or walked by it every day, and it comforted them. They saw Lucille and the girls out on the porch or caught a glimpse of them in the yard and it charmed them and made them feel like they could manage the worst the world had to offer. The sheriff had to absorb the impact of every tragedy in the county, and yet look at his little girl there, her face shining with hair flashing gold in dappled rays of sun.

When the *Beaufort Gazette* called him the "Boy Sheriff," in the uncontested election of 1938, it would be for the last time.

Despite the intensity of his work, Ed McTeer wrote that his sheriff's blood drove him to take risks that included "a friendly game once a week." One particular night he lost so bad he thought somebody must've put a root on *him*. He wrote that when he got home he crawled into bed without waking his wife. The next morning he saw all three girls standing over him dressed in their Sunday best. Lucille stood behind them, holding his pants by the cuffs and shaking. She realized what happened. She told the girls that their father had lost all his money and they didn't have Sunday School money this week. "I'll make sure you have it from now on," she said.[142]

Ed did not go church with them that day. He later wrote that when the collection plate came around, the two older girls simply nodded solemnly and passed the plate along. "No family skeleton would be revealed by them. They knew the score," Ed wrote. But Sally, the five year old, got up and walked into the aisle. "Straightening her dress, she announced in a loud voice, 'We have nothing to give the Lord today. Daddy lost his and the Lord's money in a poker game last night.'"[143]

Ed and Lucille had a son in September of 1938, James Edwin McTeer, III. Of course, Ed doted on his daughters, and he had taught them about the outdoors, but a son! Ed was delighted. His mother Florence didn't move in after all, but she was able to meet her new grandson before she went down to St. Francis Hospital in Charleston. After suffering there for several weeks, she went to her daughter Louise's to die. She had given Ed and Louise the sight. She was a spiritual woman and a Christian and she had thought about dying. She had always told her children that all protestant churches would get them into heaven, but the Episcopal Church was the first class Pullman Coach. She liked going first class. She told her daughter that she was ready to go. She died.

The *Gazette* reported that it was one of the biggest funerals Beaufort had ever seen. "Cars were lined up for a mile and people could not get in the house." Eight highway patrol cars were on the street. Deputy Randall and Arthur Paul were among the active pallbearers. Senator Harvey, Representative Thomas, Deputy Cooler, Deputy Koth, and the Mayor of Beaufort all acted as honorary pallbearers.[144]

They laid her in the ground in the cemetery only a few blocks from her son's new home. People dropped flowers on the grave until the fresh dirt was completely covered with overlapping bursts of color, creating a floral skin for the raw earth.

Chapter 26

McTeer's mother and father were both gone and along with them, a connection to the world as it had been. It was his world now. He was sheriff and a root doctor too, a self-made messiah of sorts. People came to him asking to be healed. They believed in him.

Others believed in his political juju. When Representative Thomas McMillan, of South Carolina's First Congressional District, died, everybody starting asking Ed to run for the open seat. McTeer told the *Gazette* he supported McMillan's wife for the job. Ed knew that he would not be happy in Washington. Why would he leave the varied and exciting life he led in Beaufort? Whatever the prestige, Congress seemed like a desk job to McTeer. And there was no good hunting or fishing up there either. No, a sheriff's blood and a sedentary life did not mix. If McTeer needed a reminder about the dangers of mixing the two, he needed look no further than his old friend Mattie Simmons.

McTeer couldn't overlook Simmons any longer. Ed had it from several sources that Mattie had been cussing him, talking about a showdown. They were on opposite sides, but they had been playing the same game for a long time and each knew the other played well. Or they had known it. A bottle cracked Mattie's skull during a bar fight and he had been messed up ever since. Ed knew Mattie wasn't thinking right. When he imagined himself unhinged like that, he cringed.

One day, he received a note from Simmons. He expected trouble. Instead, it said that there were twelve wild turkeys out on the Simmons place; he asked the sheriff to meet him there on Saturday morning.

When he wrote about it later, McTeer reported that Lucille didn't understand. "You certainly are not going, are you?" she asked.[145]

Ed recalled his reply. "Why of course I'm going. Mattie is a true sportsman. I'll be safer in the woods as his guest than I would be in the courthouse," he said. "Now if I was going as sheriff," he added, "that would be another story."[146]

Out at the Simmons place, Mattie put Ed in the blind and told him to shoot two birds. He was going to check out some other spots and wanted Ed to get one for him, too.

Ed was ready when the world erupted from dark at dayclean. McTeer heard the beep of a gobbler. It was a giant bird. His trigger finger itched he wanted that bird so badly. But Mattie had said there would be a flock of twelve. Ed did not shoot the big bird, but waited on the flock.

Soon enough, they arrived. The birds were beeping fast and close. Gunfire tore the morning like a strip of wrapping paper. McTeer hit two birds with one shot. Mattie returned. Ed told him about the "monster bird."

"Man," Mattie said, "you missed the chance of a lifetime to kill Old Two-toes. . . That turkey has come out of more close calls than anything I've ever hunted. He just out-thinks you. I'm glad you didn't kill him though," Ed recalled Mattie's words. "Because he and I have a date and I want to hang that beard and foot on my wall."[147]

The next week, the sheriff found another note from Simmons: "Dear Sheriff, the next time you come to Bluffton come prepared. I mean it."[148]

Simmons knew McTeer would come to Bluffton: he couldn't ignore such a threat. And now that he was going after Simmons as the sheriff, it *was* another story. McTeer probably didn't tell Lucille that he was going to Bluffton to "see who the lucky one would be."[149]

McTeer could think of no one worse to be in a shoot out with than Mattie Simmons. He had seen Simmons "make shots with both rifle and shotgun that seemed impossible." It would be a true contest.

He pulled up in front of Mattie's store in his police car and got out. The streets were empty, uncanny. Ed steeled himself. He ran in to the store, hoping to catch Simmons by surprise.[150]

Simmons was slouched over behind the counter, with a pistol in his lap—soused. He was so wasted that he didn't even recognize the sheriff when he busted in the door. McTeer took him in and sent him down to Columbia for a psychiatric evaluation.

Friends were hard to keep over the course of a long career. Ed also had a run in with his old friend State Representative Calhoun Thomas, when Thomas, the chair of the House Judiciary Committee, supported a bill that would introduce a state police system (an idea vocally supported by Governor Maybank). The bill would create a police commission that consisted of the governor, attorney general, and adjunct general. The Police Commission would have its own state wide police force. It reminded McTeer of the old rural police system writ-large. He vigorously opposed the plan. He and the other sheriffs—of whose association he was still president—felt that the bill would limit the authority, effectiveness and autonomy of the sheriff's office. McTeer said that the state police system should be "kept on the road"—functioning as a highway patrol. McTeer told a House Panel that "there has been some talk of gangsters penetrating our state," creating the need for a state-wide force. "I challenge that. They wouldn't live in South Carolina five minutes. If they came to Beaufort County and I didn't kill them a storekeeper would. They need congested areas. Give us high class detectives under the Governor. . . Not men who will insult our sheriffs." Thomas, one of the bill's authors, asked for more input from the sheriff. The proposal was dropped.[151]

Chapter 27

After a decade in office, ghosts swarmed around McTeer's head, whether he could see them or not. Fourteen years after the murder of rural policeman Paul Carden, Sheriff J.E. McTeer, Jr. was informed that the Ohio State police had captured Ben Hayward, the brother of the man they'd caught and executed seven years earlier. The *Gazette* gave McTeer credit. "The sheriff traced Heyward from Pittsburgh to Canada and back to Cleveland, Ohio, where he was captured which was a fine piece of work on the sheriff's part. But Ed never gives up a case."[152]

McTeer got a car ready. He got the solicitor Randolph Murdaugh, and Deputy Hubert Randall, who had carried Carden's body back to the car under fire. They drove to Cleveland to bring Heyward back. Heyward "put up a stiff fight" against extradition. He told the Ohio authorities that he'd had trouble with the Beaufort police in a race riot. There were three different hearings and a meeting with the governor before the extradition was approved. Randall sat in the back with Heyward. They reminded Ben Heyward what his brother Willie had said: it was Ben who killed Carden and shot at Randall. It could not have been a pleasant ride for Heyward.

The unofficial story in the Beaufort County Sheriff's Office was that the Governor of Ohio had changed his mind at the last minute and rescinded the extradition papers. But the sheriff had already left with his prisoner. The governor sent the state highway patrol after McTeer, to catch him before he reached the state line. Ed had an idea what was happening. He hit the gas when he saw the troopers. If he didn't stop, they couldn't deliver the new papers. They flashed their lights; he kept going. They chased him right up until the state line where they had to let it go.

Some people said the Ohio police wanted to charge the South Carolina sheriff with kidnapping.

The facilities at the county jail had been substantially improved since 1932 and McTeer held Heyward there until his trial. He was electrocuted on 26 April 1940. McTeer had concluded the last unfinished business from his father's era. He went out and looked at his parents' graves. He came home and looked at his children in the big white house, at his wife, harried with the four of them, but beautiful. It was a new decade, a new era, a new world.

He didn't know whether the new world was a *better* world or not when Mattie Simmons' store burned down. Mattie had just got back from Columbia. When the store caught fire, he wasn't able to escape but "died in the flames while sleeping."[153] We all end up making goofer dust, but that was no way to go. It was 1941 and the last of the old-time rough and tumble men were dead. Well, the next to last. For Ed McTeer had discovered that like the root doctors, he was a bridge between different worlds.

December 7, 1941: The Japanese bombed Pearl Harbor. Beaufort could not remain isolated. Ed McTeer joined the Beaufort County Council of Defense—part of the larger State Council of Defense. He organized the county's air raid defense procedures and was appointed Coordinator of Civilian Defenses by the governor. In 1942, the thirty-nine year old McTeer was called upon by his old friend Juan Ceballos to serve as Executive Officer in the newly formed United States Coast Guard Beach Patrol. Ceballos, one of the wealthy Northerners who owned plantations in the Beaufort area, was the commander of the patrol. He wanted Ed because of his knowledge of the coast and the islands. The Coast Guard was afraid German subs would take advantage of the same geographical features that made Beaufort so attractive to rum smugglers in the twenties. Nobody knew those features like Ed McTeer.

On 16 October 1942, the governor gave McTeer leave for the duration of the war and appointed Hubert Randall sheriff. Ceballos soon took over the Office for War Bonds allotment. McTeer became Commander of the Beach Patrol. The Coast Guard had more than McTeer's local knowledge in mind. An article describing his appointment noted that he was well known as a "criminologist, finger-print and handwriting expert, boatman, rifle marksman and horseman" and other documents declared him an expert on "seed ticks, rattle snakes, surface water and hurricanes." [154] His command extended from Wilmington, North Carolina, to Jacksonville, Florida.

The Coast Guard commandeered cabins built by the Civilian Conservation Corps for the state park on Hunting Island in the thirties. They were used as offices and barracks for McTeer's men. His unit patrolled the beaches with horses and specially trained German Shepherds.

The unit saw little action. McTeer got reports that a German submarine surfaced at Coffin Point on St. Helena Island. A sub was later captured nearby. It was loaded with fresh fruits and vegetables believed to have come from the island. That was the extent of engagement with the enemy.

McTeer knew that the boredom could crush the men. To guard is to wait, most of all. McTeer wanted his men sharp when they were on patrol, which meant they had to be occupied, somehow, when they were not. He managed to procure twenty thousand dollars worth of recreational equipment. He got ping pong, pool tables, phonographs, and books and put them in Red Cross Recreational Cabins. These cabins were not standard issue.

Commander McTeer also organized a boxing team. He had been interested in the "sweet science" since Gerald's run as a fighter back in the 'teens. His interest was revived when he trained Zeke, who fought in several bouts at the armory before the war. In the Coast Guard, Ed became friends with former heavyweight champion Jack Dempsey. Dempsey had been running a nightclub in New York and during the war he was made a Lieutenant Commander in the Coast Guard. He organized and refereed boxing exhibitions for the enlisted men. Dempsey would come to town, stay with the McTeers on Bay Street, and referee matches. Dempsey called one of McTeer's young light heavyweights "the best ring prospect he had seen in some years."[155]

McTeer's Coast Guard regiment boxed other Guard teams,fought the Marines from Parris Island, and competed in the Golden Gloves competition. McTeer was the Commanding Officer and Paul "County" Ferguson was the coach and trainer of the team. In 1943, the team only lost twice. The *Post and Courier* called the squad the "most effective team of amateur boxing on the eastern seaboard." It was not surprising, since "boxing, judo, and other commando tactics are high up on the classroom list of subjects for members of the Mounted Beach Patrol."[156]

Beaufort celebrated Navy Day on 27 October 1943. A parade began at four o'clock that afternoon, starting at City Hall and making its way down Bay Street—lined with people—until it hit the high school. The Marine Corps had two bands and the Naval Air Station had one too. The marching music blared. Tubas, trombones, and well-shined shoes glittered in the sun. McTeer's Beach Patrol walked with twenty dogs, as erect and controlled as soldiers. The crowd cheered for the dogs—the only Germans getting cheers that year. A battalion of Marines marched along with them, every foot in step, every breath in disciplined time. Sailors from the air base followed in perfect formation. Then there was the heavy equipment people really came to see, the "jeeps, anti-aircraft equipment, amphibian trucks, and other army vehicles."[157]

There was a boxing match, which Dempsey refereed. The greatest rivalry was between the Beach Patrol and the Marines. The Marines defeated McTeer's team. It was an embarrassing defeat, but they had a hell of a team. Everybody could see that. They'd be ready next year.

Chapter 29

During the War, the Draft Board found that an unusual number of young men from Beaufort were unfit for service due to health conditions. Scores of Lowcountry blacks came in for their physicals with heart palpitations. On 26 October 1943, a segregated bus headed to Fort Jackson, where the black inductees would have physicals. According to Samuel Hopkins Adams, who wrote about the case for *True Magazine*, a "youth named Crispus Green assured his family of his prompt return." He told them: "Mr. Big in Washington ain' go'n get me foh his wah. Dr. Buzzard fix me up." Others had similar stories. "Sam Graves bragged to his friends that Dr. Bug had sold him a sure charm against military service." The whole bus seemed to be rooted. According to Adams the draftees broke out in song: "Ain' gonna study wah no mo." The song, Adams wrote, "was punctuated by frequent applications to the root medicine flasks which many of them carried." According to Adams' account, "Before Columbia was reached Crispus Green and Sam Graves were dead." Several others were rushed to the hospital. When the FBI took over the investigation, they contacted Lieutenant Commander McTeer to consult with him about the deaths.[158]

McTeer briefed the agents on rootwork and its local practitioners. He gave a certain respect to Dr. Buzzard, but afforded no such deference to Dr. Bug, whose real name was Peter Murray. McTeer characterized Murray as an illiterate opportunist, and an "upstart." Murray had no mantle. Instead, "with a small cash outlay for purple glasses, a stuffed owl, and some other mystical objects, he began a practice right in his home."[159]

Adams described Dr. Bug as "a squat, shambling, dull-eyed, timorous old man." His clients were "young men in stalwart health whose condition . . . after treatment, deteriorated rapidly." McTeer obtained some potion from a draft reject. The man claimed he forgot who gave it to him.

The Feds analyzed the potion, which turned out to be arsenate of lead dissolved in moonshine. Doctors confirmed that such a mix would cause the "hippity hoppity heart" that had saved the young men from the draft. They searched the local pharmacies until they found one with a large order for arsenic. The order was marked with a scrawl: Peter Murray.[160]

Adams wrote that Dr. Bug spoke "a dialect so sparse in consonants" that only Sheriff McTeer could understand him.[161]

McTeer and two FBI agents drove out to Peter Murray's shack on the Broad River at Laurel Bay. They entered and showed him their warrant. He sat quietly in a corner and watched them through purple sunglasses. One agent opened a wooden trunk. Inside, he found crumpled up bills. They counted out tens, twenties, and hundreds—over three thousand dollars altogether. The other agent found some medicine bottles and McTeer spotted the jug of moonshine. Dr. Bug sat there until they found the arsenic; then he confessed.

McTeer asked Dr. Bug if he knew that it was against the law to keep boys out of the draft. "Nossir," Dr. Bug replied. "If a boy got no call to study war, nobody got a right to force him."[162]

Dr. Bug was arrested but he was not charged with the deaths of Crispus Green and Sam Graves. McTeer often said the medical examiner wondered how a man of Peter Murray's education had calibrated the arsenic so that his patients didn't die.

Murray was tried in Federal Court and convicted of practicing medicine without a license. He was sentenced to one year in jail or a thousand dollar fine. Mr. Murray offered to pay the fine, in cash. The same trunk was brought into the courthouse for the doctor. It contained $7,025. Dr. Bug counted out a thousand and paid his fine, then got up and walked out the door. An IRS agent, who was calculating figures at the back of the courtroom, nabbed Murray on his way out. The IRS took $2,080.77. Murray claimed he had never heard of the agency. Soon after meeting the taxman, Peter Murray died.[163]

Meanwhile, Lieutenant McTeer and his coach, County Ferguson could not agree on which fighters should represent the team at the next year's Golden Gloves. They each had their own observations, theories and philosophies. Each would listen without conceding. They bickered and cajoled. The press covered the quarrel. McTeer was skilled in persuasion, but County Ferguson would not budge. They argued and fought and sometimes it seemed like they might come to blows. McTeer must have respected Ferguson's opinion because he didn't pull rank and order the coach to obey him. The team that resulted from what *Post and Courier* sports writer Doug Donehue dubbed the "Compromise of '44" traveled to New York for the Golden Gloves tournament and "blasted their way to seven of the fifteen championships in the open and novice divisions of the competition." One of their welterweights was "voted outstanding boxer in the tournament," and another was voted most popular. They were, in fact, the most popular boxing team to ever fight in the Lowcountry.[164]

Since Ed McTeer's command extended from North Carolina to Florida, he was often away from Beaufort. But he was home enough for Lucille to become pregnant again. There were already four children running around the house. Ed III, the youngest, was six and about to start school. Sally was ten and Georgiana and Jane were fourteen and fifteen years old. Running that household was a tough job for a pregnant woman, especially with a part time husband and a war on. But, like most middle class white families, she had a black woman to help her cook and clean.

At the same time, the federal government turned to McTeer again. Agents were ready to bring a case against Stephaney Robinson. They'd found a young man ready to testify that "he had paid Dr. Buzzard ten dollars for a conjure guaranteed to help him out of the service." The witness was brought to a private meeting at the courthouse. McTeer had seen too many witnesses freak out on the stand; he wanted to see if this young man could handle it, so they brought Dr. Buzzard in as well. They asked the witness if Mr. Robinson was the man to whom he had given the money. Dr. Buzzard, "tall, slender, calm, implacable, dignified, imperceptibly turned his head toward the perspective witness." The young man "began to pluck frantically at his shoulders, breast and knees."[165]

When one of the FBI agents asked the kid what was wrong with him, he told them he was "breshin off the spells." Dr. Buzzard took off his dark glasses and stared at the witness, who started sweating. He mumbled. He cried. He choked and finally puked onto the office floor. He said that this was not the Dr. Buzzard he had been talking about.[166]

The FBI decided to give up their investigation. A rough and ready new deputy in Hubert Randall's force picked up where they left off.

Courthouse records show that O.C. Michael swore "on the 30th day of December, 1943, that upon information and belief one Stephaney Robinson did violate section 516 code of S.C. Law and Willie J. Turner is a material witness to prove" it, he arrested Dr. Buzzard. A *Beaufort Gazette* article, dated 13 January 1944, declared: "Dr. Buzzard Arrested." The article was short and read in total: "Stephaney Robinson, better known as Dr. Buzzard Negro living on Lady's Island was arrested last week by Sheriff Randall and charged with practicing medicine without a license. He posted bond to appear at next term of court."

Adams wrote that since Dr. Buzzard had been arrested "two courses were open to him. With his money he could easily afford the fee of a fellow practitioner." A root doctor made a lot of his money in court, and Dr. Buzzard was the best of the courtroom doctors. He'd often said that the law of the court was no match for a properly chewed root. His friends and family reminded him of this. He could hire a brother doctor to chew a root for him. Dr. Buzzard just shook his head. Instead, he hired State Senator Brantley Harvey—the best defense lawyer in town.[167]

The court charged that he "willfully and unlawfully practiced medicine or surgery in the state." Arthur Paul, McTeer's fishing buddy, was the Grand Jury foreman. Their verdict read: "The judge of the law and sentence of the court: That you, Stephaney Robinson, be confined to the state penitentiary or on the public works of Beaufort County or in the jail of said county for a period of three months or pay a fine of three hundred dollars."

Robinson paid the fine, in cash. According to Adams, "Senator Harvey still maintains, not without reason, that his client was victimized on unproved suspicion of having been implicated in the draft-dosing, that the medical charge was a pretext, and that he had been punished for what the root brotherhood had been doing with impunity for generations."[168]

Brantley Harvey Jr., who took over his father's practice, recalled that Dr. Buzzard paid his father with crumpled up dollar bills stored away in an old trunk in the corner of the room.

Samuel Hopkins Adams concluded that the Federal Root Doctor in Washington, "Mr. Big," put a root on Dr. Buzzard and defeated him. Roger Pinckney XI, a writer and son of Beaufort's long-time Coroner, saw it the other way around. In his mind, Dr. Buzzard helped Mr. Big in Washington and brought about the end of the war. In *Blue Roots*, Pinckney wrote that "all the young men who went to root doctors hoping to end the war before their own inductions resulted in the atomic bomb."[169]

Chapter 31

The threat to the Sea Islands was gone long before Hiroshima and Nagasaki. On 12 October 1944, South Carolina Governor Olin B. Johnston wrote to Ed McTeer that it had been brought to his attention that McTeer's unit (which he described as the Lookout System) had been decommissioned. He commended McTeer for the "splendid job," he'd done, but added that McTeer was "very much needed" in his position as sheriff. "I feel that with your experience of sixteen years in office as sheriff, it would be most desirable for you to agree to assume this office so as to help me and other officials in making preparations to face the many issues which will confront us when peace is again had."

The decommissioned unit did not get the chance to outbox the Marines on Navy Day that October. Ed McTeer was discharged. He returned to reive his old shire and to greet his new son, Thomas McTeer, who had been born in August. When Ed returned, an article in the paper reported "the well known and popular young Beaufort man will be welcomed back home by his friends throughout the county." It quoted him saying he would be glad to be back home in Beaufort and resume his duties as sheriff.

Lucille and Ed and the five children could be seen through the window of the Bay Street home basking in the warmth of return. Hubert Randall had done a fine job. After so many years as a deputy, he could feel good about the job he had done as sheriff. But he had not won an election and he knew he could not. He stepped down and welcomed Ed back.

According to McTeer, neither Mr. Big in Washington, nor O.C. Michael put Dr. Buzzard out of commission. Even after the war, McTeer wrote, "Many times, I've looked back into the courtroom and seen the purple sunglasses staring at me as Stephaney 'chewed the root' on me."[170] The root doctor sat in the courtroom and stared and chewed until spit and dribble rolled down his chin. Or he left powders, tokens or pieces of dead animals in the courtroom or in the offices or mailboxes of witnesses and prosecutors. Solicitor Randolph Murdaugh claimed that when he started prosecuting cases he often found "little packages of things on my desk, like the leg of a chicken and some dirt and feathers and things and at first I didn't know what they were and I'd throw them in the trash bag. And one day, I was talking to Sheriff McTeer, I said, 'Ed what are these things I keep finding on my desk?' He said 'somebody's trying to put a spell on you… to keep you from convicting the person.' Of course, I started collecting them as mementos then." Murdaugh did not know of any time when such tactics have worked though he acknowledged: "I have had people refuse to come testify and it may be that they had a spell put on them and they believed it."[171]

McTeer returned to the courtroom one day to find white powder dusting all the official desks. He got the bailiff to clean up the powder, then asked Robinson into the hallway. He reported the conversation that followed: "'Stephaney,' I said. 'I don't mind you chewing a root on me; I don't care if you chew your teeth down to your gums. But the next time you put root powder on our desks the judge will root you with a sentence of ninety days."

Robinson "just grinned and said, 'Don't talk so loud, man. I'm going to bring you two fine chickens.'" Two weeks later, McTeer found two white chickens cackling on his porch. [172]

But he told another version of the same story. This time, the doctor didn't get the cool line "Don't talk so loud, man." Instead he was stuck with a laconic, "I hear you."[173]

And he didn't conjure up chickens for the court room business, either. McTeer wrote: "Word came to me that I was pushing Dr. Buzzard too hard and that he was going to bring me down." McTeer's response? "I told my informer that I was a witchdoctor also and that we would see who's powers are strongest. 'Tell Buzzard that trouble is close to him. I don't like to be threatened.'"[174]

In one account, the sheriff then went out to shoot the buzzards that perched above the courthouse, as a symbolic gesture. McTeer took aim with his rifle and fired. He killed the birds. The next day, he climbed up to the top of the tower to dispose of the carcasses, and discovered that the dead buzzards had blown into the town's water tank, contaminating the whole thing.[175]

A bad omen, but the fates favored the sheriff. "Some bad things happened to their families that I got credit for," McTeer told a newspaper reporter.[176] In his own books, McTeer reported that Dr. Buzzard's son "ran his car off the causeway during a rainstorm and drowned." McTeer wrote that not long after the accident, "I drove up in my backyard and Dr. Buzzard was sitting in his car waiting for me. 'I've brought you two fine chickens, let's you and me be friends.'"

McTeer went on to claim that Dr. Buzzard told him "I've got the power and so do you, I can tell. I won't give any more medicine. I'll just deal with spirits."

McTeer told Dr. Buzzard that he would give up "black" witchcraft. He only wanted to help people from now on. Dr. Buzzard said he was getting old. He wanted to share his secrets. He and the sheriff wouldn't interfere with one another anymore. The money, Dr. Buzzard said, was in putting spells on people, so he'd keep on doing that. "You take them off. . . ." He flashed a defiant grin at McTeer. "If you can."

McTeer claimed that he and Dr. Buzzard "joined forces." Dr. Buzzard taught the Sheriff his father's African secrets. When Dr. Buzzard accepted him, McTeer's "prestige in this exclusive society was magnified many times." The prestige enabled him to accomplish his plan: Sheriff McTeer was now a white witch doctor. "White," he often explained, "because I remove spells. Not because of the color of my skin."[177] He had united the legal and spiritual authority in Beaufort County. And he finally solved one of the problems that had vexed him ever since he took over as sheriff twenty years before: "Dr. Buzzard kept his word and no longer gave medicine."[178]

Chapter 32

Dr. Buzzard had always been a legend. But over time, the stories proliferated. There was never a single buzzard, always a wake. "Dr. Buzzard," McTeer would exclaim. "He was the greatest!"[179] Buzzard, he wrote, "brought the art to the point of perfection."[180] These claims now bolstered McTeer's own authority. After defeating Dr. Buzzard, he claimed: "I was number one."[181] The idea stuck. "McTeer and Buzzard was like that," said an eighty-one year-old Gullah man, crossing his fingers. "They used to say, 'What Dr. Buzzard know, Sheriff McTeer want to learn.'"

I'd see just how pervasive the legend was while interviewing a former FBI agent named Denny March in my car at the Beaufort Post Office one hot August day. March was telling me about the attempts people made to root him over the years. "I was a New Yorker, Federal Agent, Roman Catholic—who the hell knows what the hell someone was coming after me for? I mean I didn't have a clue what kind of people believed in that crap until I found out that a lot of people did and was shocked." He interrupted himself and pointed at a black man walking by. "There's a guy you should talk to right here. Grab this guy. This guy's a character." March rolled down the window. He yelled out: "Hey Nathanial!"

Nathanial approached the car, squinting at us. He was a short, dark-skinned man in a gray t-shirt. His hair was the same length as the beard and thin mustache on his face. It sparkled a little with sweat. He had friendly eyes. "He your son?" he asked March. The agent shook his head.

"What you know about the root?" March asked Nathanial with his thick New York accent. Nathanial didn't say anything. "The root?" March repeated.

"Oh," Nathanial understood now. "You have to believe in it to work. It's a mind over matter thing," Nathanial said. "I don't believe in none of that," he added. He looked in the car. "You guys going back to Lady's Island?"

Agent March lived there. He said: "I'll take you. But you got to wait a little." He smiled. "You know anything else about the root though? Huh?"

Nathanial shook his head.

I asked, "You know anything about Sheriff McTeer?"

Nathanial smiled. "He pretty good. He better than Dr. Buzzard. I ain't lying," he assured me, almost laughing now, hunched over a little. "He better than Dr. Buzzard." Then he surprised me by reaching into the window, over March, and knuckle-bumping me.

March laughed. Even he seemed intrigued. "Oh you knew Buzzard?" he asked.

"Course," Nathanial said. "Buzzard's my sister's daddy."

"Buzzard's your sister's daddy?" asked March, incredulous.

"Yeah, I'm not lying. McTeer's good," Nathanial said. He was still laughing. He said that was all he knew. It was 105 degrees and March told him to wait for him in the Post Office where it's cool. "I'll be done in a minute. I have to get my mail. I'll come in and I'll give you a ride home."

I thanked Nathanial and he walked off through the heat waves rising up from the asphalt.

"He's a disabled veteran. Viet Nam," March said. "Shot in the back and every time I see him I give him a couple bucks. He doesn't take drugs and he's always clean. Nice guy."

I saw Nathanial around town. I didn't quite believe that he knew Dr. Buzzard or that the doctor was his sister's father. But I liked him and I always gave him five bucks. One time, I asked him to clarify. We were standing on Bay Street, across from the Best Western, just before the street opens up and becomes residential. From there you can just see the bay past the end of the solid line of storefronts that would feel Midwestern if not for the thick soft burn of salt in the air.

"Dr. Buzzard is really your sister's father?"

"Yeah, yeah. Gregory. That's her name. She's in Atlanta. Her last name. You can look her up."

McTeer claimed that he received Dr. Buzzard's mantle, but there was a second Dr. Buzzard, Robinson's son-in-law, who people called Buzzy. But his name was W.T. Gregory. He died in the late 1990s. "Gregory, huh?" I said.

He nodded. "Gregory. In Atlanta."

"Thanks, Nathanial" I said.

"I'm not kidding about McTeer," Nathanial said. "He was good."

Dr. Buzzard died in 1947 of stomach cancer. He was eighty-seven years old. Some say the juice from the roots he chewed all those years caused the cancer. Others say the root doctors divided his body. If so, McTeer got the best part: the myth. Once Buzzard was gone there was no one to contradict McTeer's claims.

Chapter 33

At the same time he was learning from Dr. Buzzard, McTeer helped a young candidate for governor. Like Ed, Strom Thurmond was a driven man. One of Thurmond's relatives said, "If Strom's elected governor, I wouldn't work for the state of South Carolina for anything on earth. He would work me to death. He believes in working all the time and he doesn't understand how other people don't share the same ideas."[182]

Thurmond was from Edgefield, in the far West of the state, south of Columbia. Edgefield was the home of the notorious Ben "Pitchfork" Tillman, one-eyed Red Shirt vigilante and radical racist governor; it was a rough-and-tumble back-country kind of place and often found itself at odds, politically, with the more refined Lowcountry. But McTeer and Thurmond were of the same generation and they seemed to like each other. Thurmond was running as a progressive New Dealer, and McTeer shared these views. He helped Thurmond raise money and created a political organization in Beaufort.

It was a weird, lawless election in 1946. The state had officially eliminated all of its election laws when the U.S. Supreme Court ruled that the all-white primaries in Texas were unconstitutional. The Democratic Party was now considered a private club. On the day of the election, a black taxi-driver in Columbia went to vote and was turned away from the polls.

When Thurmond won the run-off after the first round of the primary, he wrote McTeer a telegram:

> I APPRECIATE YOUR EXCELLENT SUPPORT PLEASE ACCEPT MY DEEPEST GRATITUDE FOR A JOB WELL DONE EXPRESS MY THANKS TO OUR FRIENDS FOR THEIR HARD WORK AND

SEND MY OFFICE A LIST OF OUR FRIENDS WHO ACTIVELY SUPPORTED ME AND A SEPARATE LIST OF CONTRIBUTORS WE WANT TO THANK THEM BY LETTER.[183]

Ed was unopposed again, and was no longer the "Boy Sheriff;" he was the High Sheriff. He knew every thing about everybody. And they knew he knew. He helped Thurmond wield influence, setting up talks and making deals.

McTeer loved the art of deal making. He began to traffic in real estate. The county government gave McTeer's name to wealthy people from other areas interested in buying property in Beaufort. McTeer's mind ever moved across the landscape, looking for the future. The world was different now, after the war. Everybody knew that. But this was only the beginning. He'd seen the future way back in the days of the hunting preserves and the nudist colony on Cat Island. He figured rich people from up North and the Midwest were going to get sick of that god-awful cold up there when they retired with all their money and they were going to want to start heading South. Tons of them were already going to Florida. But here was the "Beautiful Beaufort by the Sea"—a phrase that Ed coined and the city adopted as its unofficial motto.

The department was changing as well. When Thurmond was elected, Zeke took a job as a state constable. Ed was proud, but hated to see his little brother go. Gerald was a different story. He was still drinking and getting too fat to be an effective deputy. People started calling him "Old Plute."

Gerald had married an eccentric woman named Zoe. She had gone to college, but had now become something of a recluse. Ed wanted to help, so he set Gerald up as the jailor. They moved into an apartment by the jail and Gerald got fifty cents a day to feed the prisoners. Most days, Gerald went to the Hunting Island Bridge with 'his' trustee. The trustee carried a stool for Gerald to sit on. He would take a live shrimp, put it on a hook with a cork, cast the line, and hand the rod to Plute who would sit there and wave at the passing cars, until the cork bobbed. Then he'd hand the rod back to the trustee, who'd reel the fish in. Plute brought the fish back. A trustee cleaned it. The prisoners ate fish and grits. Gerald pocketed the fifty cents. They say he was so fat that the trustee had to tie his shoes.

In the meantime, Ed promoted O.C. Michael to Chief Deputy. Everybody called him Mike. Mike was a large, formidable man with a reputation. Some called him hot-headed. Others said he was brutal. The Gullah did not trust him as they trusted McTeer. But when trust didn't work, McTeer also used fear. He didn't hex people, but he didn't mind if some thought he did. "I firmly believe that many of the criminals I arrested while I was sheriff were more afraid of the harm I could do them as a witch doctor, with the power of black root on them, than the power of the law," he wrote. "It served my purpose to let this belief stand."[184]

McTeer, wanting to arrest someone for distilling moonshine, drove out to the man's house. He parked in the yard and got out of the car. He saw someone peek out through the window. He walked around the house three times, mumbling and chanting all the while. He got back in the car, slammed the door, and drove away. The next morning the man was waiting for him at the jail when he got to work.

There were other root doctors: Dr. Eagle in town, Dr. Snake on the island, and Dr. Crow in Burton, but none had the authority of McTeer. He was looking spookier as he aged. He still had wide shoulders, long legs, and huge hands, but his features had grown more intense as their lines were both blurred and deepened by the years. His face was cast in shadow by a Panama hat, which had replaced his old fedora.

This spiritual authority certainly helped him enforce the county's laws. Ed told a reporter for the *Gazette*: "I was sitting on my porch about two o'clock in the afternoon when I noticed an old negro man with a young boy around twenty years old coming up the steps. As they reached the top of the steps the old man asked 'Was this the sheriff?' I told him yes. He said 'Mr. McTeer, I want to give you my boy.' I asked what was wrong with him. He said 'he commit murder and I say I gonna take you to de Sheriff, so here we is.'

"The old man said the boy had killed a man at Daufuskie Island the night before, that he made him get in a boat and they had been thirteen hours making the trip in a rowboat, traveling all night and up to that hour reaching town. They left the boat at Port Royal and walked five miles."

The old man went over to the jail with his son and the sheriff. McTeer asked Gerald and Zoe to feed the man and give him some leftovers for the long, lonely trip across the Calibogue sound. Just before leaving his son the man said: "Well son, I am going back to the island and try to raise some money and get you a lawyer."[185]

Chapter 34

In July 1947, a Federal Judge in Charleston heard the case of the black taxi driver who had been turned away from the polls in Columbia. The Court followed Justice Thurgood Marshall in arguing that the Democratic Party served a political—and therefore public—function, whether the state had election laws or not. The Party could not discriminate.

Thurmond maintained his ties with Beaufort's sheriff. Ed wrote to Thurmond on 31 July 1947. A week later, Thurmond replied: "It was so nice of you to let us use the cottage for the week beginning August 10, and we are looking forward to being down there at that time. We shall bring a couple of servants, probably a negro man and a negro woman." Thurmond's letter went on to discuss speaking engagements that Ed was helping arrange for him in Beaufort.

A photographer snapped a photo of McTeer and Thurmond: The two thirty-four year old men striding with destiny and purpose down the sidewalk. Strom stiff and serious; Ed, several inches taller with broader shoulders, laughing, a fish dangling by his side.

Shortly after Thurmond's trip to Beaufort, Harry Truman's Committee on Civil Rights demanded reform. The Committee sought to enact Federal laws that prohibited discrimination at the polls and the workplace. It wanted to outlaw poll taxes and loyalty oaths and wanted to make lynching a Federal crime.

Thurmond, once a fervent supporter of Truman, had not seemed particularly concerned with racial issues before. When the Committee for Civil Rights report came out, he became the champion of segregation. He said: "Don't forget that the so-called Civil Rights program would bring about the end of segregation in the South, forcing mixing of the races in our hotels, in our restaurants, in our schools, in our swimming pools, and in our public places. This change in our customs is not desired by either the white or colored race."

Thurmond went on: "To bring this about, the federal government would set up a super police force with power to rove throughout the states and keep our people in constant fear of being sent to a federal jail unless we accept the decrees turned out by a bunch of anti-Southern bureaucrats in Washington."[186] This was exactly the kind of thing that could get to McTeer: an enlarged version of the Rural Police system. McTeer feared a federal force would diminish his authority and effectiveness.

Thurmond became the States' Rights Party candidate for President—a so-called Dixiecrat. The South Carolina Sheriff's Association adopted a resolution that "endorsed the ideals, policies, and program of the States' Rights Party." The resolution stated: "The so-called national democratic party at the 1948 convention in Philadelphia adopted a platform under the guise of civil rights which among other things would establish an enormous national police system of almost unlimited power."

The resolution went on: "Whereas sheriffs, the chief enforcement officers of various counties, are interested in and responsible for the peace, happiness, and general welfare of all the people under their jurisdiction" and "whereas adoption and enforcement of so-called civil rights program would result in chaos, hatred, lawlessness, and bloodshed through attempting to force on now peaceful whites and Negroes without any choice of their own to work side by side."[187]

Chapter 35

Ed had now been in office for twenty-two years. Jane, his oldest daughter, had married and in 1948 birthed a daughter of her own; the "Boy Sheriff" was now a grandfather. He was also becoming something of a tycoon. He was the head of a committee to restore the historic Lafayette Building. He resigned from the Beaufort Realty Company and started his own company, working out a deal that gave him exclusive rights to sell the Coffin Point Plantation on the northernmost point of St. Helena. Cameron, the Secretary of War under U.S. Grant, bought the plantation as a vacation home half a century earlier. He sailed up to the plantation every year, giving speeches and holding lavish parties. Dancing girls scratched their initials in the windowpanes with diamonds the Senator gave them. You could still see the rough impressions nearly fifty years later. Cameron's festivities made the Pleasant Point parties of Ed's early days as sheriff seem like church socials.

Cameron died in 1918. The property had since been managed and preserved by a trust, but Cameron's heirs were ready to get rid of it now. Ed started showing it to prospective buyers, driving them around in the sheriff's car, chain smoking, talking, telling them old stories about the island.

An article in the *Gazette* noted that the Federal-style "'Big House' of old plantation days has stood empty but has been scrupulously cared for these many years. About every other year it was given a fresh coat of colonial yellow paint but the color has been changed to white within the last three years. The house is huge and rambling, containing three stories and large verandas front and back."[188] This was on the waterfront with a piazza in the back overlooking the St. Helena sound. You could see Edisto island from there, dark and heavy like the back of a turtle. The house lounged, palatial, at the end of the majestic, mile long, cathedral-like Avenue of Oaks. The large home was dwarfed by the sound and the oaks and the six hundred and fifty acres of land that surrounded it. You could divide it into lots with plenty of waterfront and keep the big house to live in and farm and still have a place of refuge.

One day, Ed was out showing the property. He was telling the client about all of these possibilities. The guy said, well then, if it's so great why don't you buy it? Ed turned the car around. When the guy asked him what he was doing, Ed told him the property had been sold. Ed dropped the guy off in town and went to the bank to borrow five thousand dollars for the down payment.[189] Coffin Point would become the capital of his empire.

The house was in good shape, but it needed to be modernized. After all, no one had lived there for nearly half a century. It didn't even have electricity. It would be a while before he moved the family in. But he could see the possibilities. He would leave behind his homemade museum filled with all his weird artifacts and his weapons collection. He could create a new cabinet of wonders on the first floor at Coffin Point. It was perfect. But he would sell the gun collection, at least part of it, to pay for a new furnace.

He had big ambitions and convict labor to bring them to fruition. He brought whole crews out in chains. They cleared brush, hacked away at palmettos and undergrowth. They dug two big holes that filled up from underground streams and provided fresh water to the farm. Then they started cutting roads.

The roads the chain gangs cut would be among McTeer's most lasting contributions. His actions had already blurred: The rumrunners and everything from the early days bled together in a sepia toned slurry. Today's actions would soon join the mix. But the lines he sketched on paper bags would remain as roads for generations.

Chapter 36

Ed McTeer prepared to move his family out to Coffin Point. But he knew that no one could ever build a plantation large enough to keep chaos out.

In February 1949, William Moseley Swain, a man described as a "Philadelphia socialite" and the grandson of the founder of the *Philadelphia Inquirer*, was found lying dead at the bottom of the steps leading to the basement of the Belfair plantation home he owned near Bluffton, South Carolina. In those days Bluffton was considered the "North's nuthouse." Wealthy families sent their less reputable members to live as "remittance men" in big plantation houses, away from the public eye. Swain was somewhat eccentric. He had been known to "fake" falling down in order to scare his friends and then amuse them when he hopped up, unscathed.

When coroner, Roger Pickney arrived, he noted: "William Moseley Swain died from the effects of a fall down stairs leading to the concrete floor of a basement." Ed McTeer wasn't so sure: "I am not satisfied that Swain did fall down the steps." They convened a coroner's inquest, everyone standing over Swain's body at the bottom of the stairs. The doctor determined "Swain had suffered a one and a half inch deep gash of the scalp and an eight inch fracture of the skull." The coroner's jury found that Swain had "died of injuries inflicted by causes undetermined."

McTeer had a cause in mind: murder. He questioned Victor Strojney, 35, a former aeronautical engineer from New Jersey who now raised cattle nearby. Strojney had been the last person known to be in the company of Swain prior to his death, and had in fact been the one to call for help from the Belfair plantation house phone that night. Strojney explained himself to McTeer—he had met up with Swain in town that morning near the bank where Swain had just secured for himself a loan of eleven thousand dollars. Swain took the opportunity to repay a personal debt of one hundred dollars to Strojney. He offered to top it with an additional six hundred dollar loan, an offer which Strojney promptly accepted. As Swain wrote a check for the total of seven hundred dollars, he invited Strojney to the Big House for drinks that evening. Pocketing the check, Strojney agreed to come over later.

They ended up having several drinks, as it turned out, and Strojney didn't make a move to depart until shortly after Swain retired. On his way out the door, Strojney claimed he heard a loud thud from within and ran back to investigate. He found Swain lying unconscious at the bottom of the stairs. When he couldn't rouse him, Strojney feared Swain was dead.[190]

McTeer didn't buy this story. First, the exchange of money didn't make sense. Why did Swain offer to loan Strojney money from the loan he had just taken out? And why would Strojney wait to leave until after Swain retired? It just didn't add up.

Then McTeer noticed a whiskey glass lying on the ground at the bottom of the stairs with Swain. If Strojney's prints were on the glass it would destroy his story: If Strojney was already out the door when Swain fell, then his glass would not have been in the basement.[191]

The prints were, indeed, Victor Strojney's. McTeer arrested him and charged him with the murder of William Mosely Swain.

Former Lieutenant Governor Brantley Harvey, Jr.'s father, the state senator, defended Strojney. The son remembered the case: "My father finally came up with the defense that Swain had fallen from the second floor on the steps and hit his head on a ledge that was out over the steps. Sheriff McTeer said that was impossible because the ledge was made so that you could go up and down under it as you ascended and descended the steps. He said, 'Aww, no. People walk up and down those steps every day.' Well, my father got a piece of cane the exact height of the man and showed that if you stood on the steps and pitched forward your head would catch on this ledge, which was where the wound was. And he was acquitted."

Harvey was good friend of the sheriff; he had recommended the governor appoint McTeer back in 1926. But they were fierce opponents in the courtroom, and neither liked to lose. There is no reference to the outcome of the case in McTeer's scrapbook.

Chapter 37

McTeer worked on his own plantation home in an attempt to keep outer darkness at bay. But he kept thinking about the Russians and the bomb. The danger of oblivion dwarfed the human crimes he contended with.

The foreboding got worse when they decided to make the super hydrogen bomb in South Carolina, on the Savannah River, a couple hours northwest of Beaufort. No one knew whether the chain reaction created by this bomb would ever stop. It could rip the entire universe apart, atom by atom. McTeer decided to build a bomb shelter at Coffin Point, but before he could get there, the bomb was brought home to Bay Street.

In 1950, the Associated Press ran a story under the headline: "S.C. Youths test First H-Bomb; Results are Drastic."

> Three young South Carolinians have tested what they call the 'world's first H-bomb. Not to be outdone by the H-bomb project coming to the Palmetto State, three young residents of Beaufort held their own experiment They mixed together certain quantities of gun powder, lard, kerosene, and flour. As the chief chemist of the project, Little Ed McTeer, Jr. was given the honor of lighting the first H-bomb. When the smoke cleared away Chief Chemist McTeer was rushed to the hospital. He suffered first degree burns. His two assistants escaped harm.[192]

I talked to "Little Ed" one day at his home at Coffin Point. "What I did was open up five or six shotgun shells. I thought when I put a match to it the thing would just flare up. Well it did flare up—around my head," he said. "I had to have a cast on my head. I was confirmed into the Episcopal Church that year, and the priest came out and performed the ceremony at the house because I had this cast on my head. Fortunately it didn't do any permanent damage. Probably scarred my mother, emotionally, though," he added.

And his father? "He was the kind of guy you just didn't want to disappoint. You just didn't want to disappoint him," he said. "He never raised a voice or a hand. Didn't have to. You know, Pat Conroy writes about all of this rage and hatred with his father. When I read that, it was so far from—I just couldn't imagine it. I'd never felt that way in my life. But you just didn't want to disappoint him."

Around the same time, a group of Ed's deputies tripped a wire out in the woods and were almost blown up as a big blast ripped the night to shreds and left a four-foot hole in the ground. The superintendent of the land had set a booby trap to catch poachers. The man was arrested—he'd nearly killed four law enforcement officers.

This incident and Little Ed's bomb accident reminded McTeer that no matter what he did to try to keep his family safe, life was an uncertain affair at best, filled with explosion, accident and malice.

Chapter 38

In 1949, a group of six state legislators were appointed to fix South Carolina's primary election laws. The *Beaufort Gazette* explained: "All primary laws were repealed in 1944 in an effort to keep Negroes from voting. Since then, however, federal courts have ruled that Negroes must be allowed to vote in all primaries. These rulings, therefore, removed the purpose for not having state primary laws."[193]

When the laws were reconfigured, Ed McTeer was the executive committeeman of the Beaufort Democratic Club and was elected a delegate. He was up for reelection in 1950. If anyone ran against him, it would be the first time in a nearly twenty-five year career as an elected official that he ever had to face black voters.

In April, N.M. Polk, a dairy farmer, announced his candidacy. At the first stump meeting at Barrel Landing, Ed said, "In a way, I am glad I have opposition this year. It will show me how I stand." He continued, "If in the twenty-four years I have served, I have not acquired the confidence of the people, I don't want the job."

The *Gazette* paraphrased the rest of McTeer's speech, reporting that he claimed he had taken only a single vacation, back in "1936 to attend the World's Fair." He did not want to keep the job for any reason other than that he was the best man for it. He urged voters to "ask the lawyers, with whom I am in constant warfare, the judges, the grand juries" about his tenure.

Polk replied: "If elected," he said, "I don't want the extra fees that go with tax executions in the sheriff's office." He said that the salary was enough to live on. "I haven't promised any jobs," he said. "But if I am elected there will be some open," implying that he would fire all of the McTeers now holding county jobs. "If you want a night watchman and process servers, you have them. If you want rigorous law enforcement then elect N.M. Polk."[194]

Later that year Polk ran a series of ads hinting that McTeer was corrupt. Polk was the candidate with "the CONCRETE PROMISE to remove all Sheriff's FEES from delinquent taxes and to neither hire, maintain, nor CRAM in office any other individual bearing the name of Polk." He concluded: "A CLEAN mind makes a CLEAN man to CLEAN up the DIRT or a CLEAN county for CLEAN people." He urged them to "GO TO YOUR POLL AND VOTE!"[195]

And they did. More people voted in the 1950 election than any election in Beaufort's history. The *Gazette* reported that McTeer "swamped his opponent" 2,199 votes to 637.[196]

Chapter 39

Blacks may have gained the power to vote in the Democratic primaries, but racial tensions were becoming an urgent issue once again. The sheriff got a call after ten o'clock one night when driver on Highway 21 in Lady's Island saw a man staggering down the road like a zombie—covered in blood, moaning, and calling for help. The passerby drove to the nearest phone and called the sheriff.

McTeer and Randall went to check it out. "When we found the stricken man," McTeer recalled, "he was lying face down, dead." He had been shot and he couldn't have made it far from the scene of the crime. They scoped out the area. McTeer noticed a car in an empty lot beside the highway. A body lay sprawled twenty-five feet from the car. Another corpse lay twisted halfway up under the vehicle, his legs sticking out. The sheriff found two .45 caliber shells by the dead man's boots.

While McTeer was examining the bodies, Deputy Randall got a call on the radio. There was witness who had escaped the shooter. He had just seen his brothers shot and was terrified. They picked him up. This was his story: He and his three brothers sang in a barbershop quartet. They had stopped in the vacant lot near the river to practice and had been working on their harmonies in the car for nearly an hour, when they noticed a black man approaching them. He started to cuss at them. Three of the singers got out of the car. One asked the black man why he was using such foul language. The man pulled out a gun and shot the boy. Another boy started to run. He was shot in the back. A third tried to crawl under the car. The man leveled the gun at him and fired. The witness never got out of the car. He crouched down and hid and the shooter never spotted him. But he didn't get a good look at the shooter either.

A crowd of angry citizens gathered. Ed had to try to control the mob while he figured out what had happened. The killer was on foot, so McTeer knew he had to live nearby. But that didn't help much. Then he remembered hearing about a veteran "who was supposed to be able to drop a rabbit at one hundred feet" with a .45. His name was Smith Harvey. When McTeer found out that Harvey lived less than a half a mile from the scene, the sheriff thought he had found his man. He and Deputy Randall drove over there, leaving Michael behind to manage the crowd.

McTeer knocked on the door. Harvey hollered out that he'd be right there. He opened the door and explained he'd been asleep. McTeer walked back to his bedroom and felt the bed: It was cold. McTeer then asked Harvey what happened. He confessed, but his story was different than the white boy's: "I was coming from a dance when I saw a parked car, but them cars park there all the time, and I didn't pay it no attention. As I walked by, one of the men leaned out and yelled, 'Where are you going, Nigger?' I told them don't call me that, and they came out of the car at me. I had my pistol, and when they came at me I shot them. I saw three men and I shot all of them."[197]

McTeer didn't know which version of the story was true. A judge and jury would decide that later. Right now he had to make sure there wasn't a fourth murder that night. He handcuffed Harvey and placed him under arrest, sending Randall to get a state trooper. When they returned, McTeer asked the trooper to take Harvey to the penitentiary in Columbia. He wrote the Governor, explaining the situation: "My county has never in its history had a lynching and I will do all in my power to see that none occurs." The Governor wrote back offering his full support. After the car had been gone an hour, McTeer told the crowd that he'd arrested a man who was already on his way to the pen in Columbia.

Most people agreed that the singers had attacked Harvey first, but McTeer and Solicitor Randolph Murdaugh weren't going to accept a self-defense plea because of the "third man." "Was he not trying to crawl under the car when he was killed?" Murdaugh asked. "If so, could he have been such a terrible threat to Harvey as to warrant his death?"

The defense attorney asked the sheriff if it was possible that the third man was shot while attacking Harvey and only crawled up under the car after he was shot. Ed testified that the placement of the cartridges at the crime scene showed that the gun had been pointing down when it was fired.

The defense questioned the sheriff's ability to make such a judgment. He asked the judge to demand a demonstration. The court went outside and crossed over Bay Street. They stood there on the riverbank in the blazing sun beneath the waving old oaks. The attorney laid out two handkerchiefs. He asked the sheriff to fire the .45 so that the shells would land on the cloth. Ed fired twice: the casings spun and landed on the handkerchiefs. Smith Harvey was convicted of murder. A short time later he was executed.[198]

Chapter 40

Blacks on the Sea Islands still talk about the Smith Harvey murder case. McTeer had treated Harvey fairly, even if he was convicted. But retaliatory violence lay like a demon behind every interracial case that came up.

A call came in one night that November. Somebody killed the postmaster out at a little village called Lobeco. When Ed and his deputies got there, they cordoned off the area. A large group of local farmers assembled. Everybody had an opinion about who did it and how the sheriff should respond and they were all shouting. McTeer "had learned many years before that a sheriff needed to get voters to be elected, no matter how efficient a detective he was," so he wasted a half an hour listening to their theories. Then "appointed the loudest of the group to guard a railroad trestle or crossroads somewhere" far away from the scene so that he could get to work.

It was an ugly scene. Mr. Wilson, postmaster and shop-keeper, was in bad shape. It looked to McTeer like more than one assailant had been at work. They had smashed Wilson's skull and his face with a club. They stuck sharp sticks through his ears. They stabbed him with an ice-pick until it broke off in his spine—twenty-nine times.

The sheriff found the lock and stock of a .22 rifle. The barrel was missing. Blood lacquered strands of the dead man's hair to the stock.

McTeer went through the books. At least thousand dollars of federal money was gone in addition to whatever the general store had earned.

Solicitor Murdaugh arrived at the scene. Randolph Murdaugh was a round man with a soft voice and big smile, when he had occasion for it. As the sun rose that morning, he had no call to smile. The crowd was restless. McTeer feared a lynching. He took the solicitor aside and told him he knew who had killed Mr. Wilson. Murdaugh said he must be joking: McTeer hadn't even left the crime scene. He told the sheriff, "Ed, you know the county and your people but I don't think this one can be solved without leaving the store."

The loudmouths outside thought transients had killed the postmaster, but it was evident to McTeer that the killers had known Mr. Wilson and his schedule. Two unemployed brothers who'd been getting in a lot of trouble lately lived nearby. McTeer told his deputies to examine the tracks. They found two sets of tracks outside. Both came and went eastward. Now McTeer knew it was the brothers. Next, he told Deputy Michael "to take as many men as he could find and search the underbrush for a depth of two hundred feet on the left side." Michael returned less than an hour later with the rifle barrel. The crowd walked back, bunched up around Michael. They were amazed. *How had the sheriff known*?

"I tried to explain," wrote McTeer, "that it was only logical that after the bullet had failed to stop Wilson, the rifle barrel had become a club and was their only remaining weapon once the pick had snapped off," he said. When they got to the woods, they would ditch it as quickly as they could. "I had guessed correctly that the man carrying the weapon was right-handed, and would have thrown the barrel to the left since that was the easiest and fastest way to dispose of it."[199]

Others saw it differently. Cases like this convinced people that the rumors about the sheriff's magical powers were true.

McTeer and Randall went to the brothers' house. They tricked the mother into telling them that the gun and the ice-pick were missing from the house. Later that same day, McTeer discovered the killers had bought two eight hundred dollar cars in Savannah. He alerted Savannah's law enforcement who found the brother's living it up at a county fair.

Chapter 41

Reason could not explain everything. McTeer and Michael had been watching a still out near Hardeeville. It was a big operation and they were waiting until the liquor was ready before they nabbed bootleggers.

When the whiskey was ready, they set up a stake-out with a Marshall from Bluffton and the Chief of Police from Hardeeville. As they trudged out into the pungent swamp just before dark, the Marshall spoke. He reminded them of an old story they'd all heard before about an itinerant peddler, who came through the area during Reconstruction days selling costume jewelry. He stopped at a nearby farm to ask for water. The family had gone to town, leaving only the teenage boy at home. He told the peddler where he could find water. The peddler put down his load. He went off for the water and the boy looked in the bag. The boy was dazzled by the jewels—he'd just found his fortune! He snuck up behind the stranger, and clubbed him in the back of the head. The man fell dead. When the boy's parents returned, they discovered his crime—and his miscalculation. They had to help their son even if it meant they lost everything for a few pieces of cut glass. They threw the body in the swamp and fled the farm. The body was eventually found and so was the family. The boy was hung; the parents charged as accessories. No one could ever live in the house again. Doors flew open. Chairs fell to the ground. Dressers slid across the floor.

Walking out through the swamp, the three law men laughed uneasily at the Marshall's story. The Marshall added that he didn't hunt around there any more because every time he went out there his dogs got spooked and wouldn't move away from where they huddled around his legs.

"Ghosts?" McTeer joked. The Marshall answered that he'd never seen a ghost, but he had heard some weird noises that he couldn't explain.

It got dark and the men took up their posts. When it was clear the bootleggers weren't going to show up, they decided to split. McTeer recalled stopping at the edge of the swamp to light a cigarette. "All at once, from the blackness of night we were bathed in an extremely bright light that seemed to cover at least four acres or more." At first they thought they'd been caught in a trap by the bootleggers. "Each of us had a different reaction; some were on their knees with pistols trying to find the source of the light; some were just crouched. . . All of us were ready to fire but there was nothing to shoot at," McTeer later wrote. The strangest thing about the light, recalled McTeer, was that it "did not shine at us but enveloped us and emanated from all directions at once, with us at the center." Suddenly, the light receded, fading away until there was nothing left but a sound that McTeer described as "a human throat's gurgling death rattle."[200]

Chapter 42

McTeer moved the family to Coffin Point in 1952. It was a paradise for the boys. He parceled out lots to his daughters as they got married, keeping his grandchildren close. Lucille had never needed to drive before. Now that they lived so far out, Ed taught her on the sandy roads. They had a maid named Renda who lived with them to help raise the children. Thomas McTeer recalled that when they moved there "an old black guy Ben Chisholm came with the plantation. He'd been there. He was born on the plantation and his parents were slaves on Coffin Point and he lived on the same little dirt floor, literally dirt. He wouldn't move. We offered him to move in various places out there, and he lived in this little one room dirt floor and I went in there many times and visited with him. He didn't talk very much but he played the juice harp. I used to love to sit and listen to him playing that juice harp. When we would have birthdays he had this white mule and he'd lead us around on this big white mule."

McTeer bought two circus ponies, Mary and Trigger, for the children. The sounds of children playing filled the air like a bright color.

McTeer had sixty hogs, a bunch of hens, and a rooster. The cattle industry was booming and he began to raise a herd of jersey cows, a Brahma cow too, and some Hereford bulls. When the cattle market collapsed, he knew it was time to move forward with his other plans.

Coffin Point was the final consolidation of McTeer's power. Cleaver Johnson, a Gullah man who was the president of the county chapter of the NAACP said, "I go to McTeer, if I had to go before the judge, cause when the judge come he go to McTeer house. And McTeer tell him what's going on, and who is who, and all that. And judge sitting on the chair in the trial, but he know from jump-street. When you give a lawyer money, the judge spin round what he want to know. When he come in this town. . . Court could be Monday and he come in Friday. He be at Mr. McTeer's house on Coffin Point all weekend."

In the early 1950s, Ed McTeer's power extended far beyond his legal jurisdiction. There were rumors that Ed McTeer was quite popular with his female constituents. Some people said he was exceptionally well-endowed. "They said the sumbitch hung to his knees," one man reported. Rumor claimed his lady admirers deeded property to him.

Sherwood Fender, a Beaufort attorney and raconteur, recalled how far the sheriff's civil authority extended. "He'd go out to the country and somebody'd say, 'Look, Mabel and I ain't getting along and we want a divorce.'

"Ed said, 'Well who married you?'

"'Well, ain't nobody married us,' the guy answered.

"Ed said, 'Ok, bring her here.' So they come by and he go through a ceremony. It might be like, 'Y'all say 'I divorce thee' three times and throw something over your shoulder.'

"And somebody'd say, 'Sheriff is that a good divorce?'

"He'd say, 'No but they didn't have a good marriage to start with either.'"

Chapter 43

McTeer's dominion was slowly disrupted by darkness. It dripped like death obliterating space and color. He had cataracts and was going blind.

The "Boy Sheriff" had become the "Blind Sheriff." He knew there would be a day when he couldn't do the job any longer. He was preparing for that, but, for the time being, he felt like he could do better blind than anyone else could do with eight eyes. Michael was a great deputy but he was too rough to be sheriff.

Randall, who had done a fine job as sheriff during the war, died in May 1953 following a brief illness. He was only forty nine. McTeer and Michael were pallbearers at the funeral.

No one ran against McTeer in 1954, but he still had to figure something out. He could neither drive nor shoot. He got his best trustee, Albert Murray, to chauffer him around. He moved Albert into the house and Albert drove Ed wherever he wanted to go. He kept an eye on Thomas, too, and helped with the other trustees who were always out on the place. Albert served lemonade at the Cub Scout meetings Lucille hosted. When dignitaries and rich northerners came down to hunt, Ed sent Albert out with them to help with the hunt. One time, these rich lawyers were out in the woods with him for the weekend and one of them asked Albert's profession. He told them that he drove for the sheriff. "Are you in jail?" the man asked. Albert allowed that he was. When the man asked what for, Albert told him. "Murder. But don't worry," he added. "It was just my wife."

Albert acted as McTeer's eyes, until it looked like the sheriff would lose his sight entirely. He went to Philadelphia for an experimental surgery and, after a six week recovery, regained some of his sight. He wore thick glasses and the visible world still appeared blurry, as if all the action in his life had permanently smudged it. But at least he could sit up on the piazza on the back of the house, above the porch, and see the sun glint off the windows on Edisto Island across the sound, marveling in the pure delight of sight.

Chapter 44

The resurgence of sight fueled McTeer's dreams of development. Convalescence renewed his hunger. When he looked off the piazza, he wanted more.

Albert drove McTeer out to Coosaw Estates on the river. The wind spun the smoke from the sheriff's cigarette. Egrets cut through the air over the marsh. McTeer studied the blurry banks of the river. He wanted to maximize the waterfront. They could cut canals to create more waterfront. It was risky, but his partner Leroy Keyserling called it visionary. The heavy equipment moved onto the island and began to cut chasms into the earth, heaving it into mounds, making way for the inevitability of water.

McTeer and Keyserling developed three other properties at the same time. McTeer tried to make others see the poetry he felt in the land. At first, as with all poetry, it had been hard to convert to money. But now, with people pouring south, it was becoming easy. He tried capture the essence of the place in short poem-like ads.

> Broad River Bluff Lots
> Exclusive deep water lots
> Facing Habersham Creek.
> This is your Chance for a
> Homesite with fishing at your door
> Lovely trees and close to Beaufort.
> Acreage also.

He signed the ad, "J.E. McTEER, REALTOR." He did not mention his other job.

Keyserling, called McTeer a "warrior statesman." But they were not alone with their big dreams and schemes for land development. Property deeds were dealt and shuffled like cards on poker night. The development of Fripp Island was the biggest game in the County. All the major money players were involved. McTeer had started the group that had run timber from the island decades earlier, but now a new group formed to turn it into a resort. They cut McTeer out of that game.

Or maybe he sat out. Even without Fripp, the market seemed endless. After the census, the state declared Beaufort the "growingest county." Retirees and military personnel promised never-ending growth potential. Everybody wanted in, including the federal government. Navy and Marine personal were stationed in the area. The military built a number of houses for them.

Suddenly there were too many houses in Beaufort. Prices dropped. People owed more than their homes were worth. The banks foreclosed on some. Others never sold and sat empty. In Charleston, people declared Beaufort "dead." Ed McTeer wrote a letter at the time to Charleston's *Post and Courier* under the title "Beaufort Today."

"The wreaths which some citizens of Charleston are laying on the County of Beaufort certainly are inappropriate at this time. The report of our demise is greatly exaggerated. If any industry was contemplating Beaufort for a site the obituaries being published in Charleston papers about our 'ghost town' would certainly be the deterrent. Congressman L. Mendel Rivers and the Marine Corps have made Beaufort the fastest growing town of its size on the Eastern Seaboard. I shudder to think of Beaufort's future if we did not have both of them. We have not sent out any S.O.S. calls. If you really want to see a beautiful and thriving town, come to Beaufort."

He signed this letter, "J.E. McTeer, Sheriff."[201]

Chapter 45

Gerald remembered when they lived at the farm on Grays Hill long before Ed got into real estate. Every evening when Ed came home, their mother said, "Edwin, empty out your pockets." Ed would dig in and come out with rocks, pinecones, arrowheads, bottle caps, shotgun shells, and other oddities. Now, Gerald must have felt a bit like Sancho Panza as he watched his brother try to put the earth itself in his pocket. Ed did not want to fight giants; he wanted to be one.

Gerald was known as the "ego-deflator" and he especially disliked "upstarts." Everyone Ed sold property to was an "upstart." Many of them frequented the Yacht Club.

The Yacht Club had nothing to do with boats. It was a private men's club on the bay. Gerald hung out there and drank, waiting for a game to pick up. Gin Rummy was the house game. The games were long, the stakes high. Eventually, some of the newer members came to Ed. They thought Gerald was cheating. He was winning all the time. They knew he could be short-tempered, so they didn't want to cause trouble, but. . . .

The sheriff agreed to talk to his brother. He went to Plute, who assured him he wasn't cheating. Those guys just didn't know how to play.

Ed remembered the last time he saw Gerald play. Plute had been sitting there day-dreaming when a rich transplant named Charlie walked in. Plute ribbed Charlie the whole time. When Charlie dealt, Plute said "You take all the shortcuts. You shortchange the pot, you don't half shuffle the cards and when you do you leave them spotted." Plute told Charlie his clothes were ridiculous. Plute said he looked like "a crane standing on one leg in a pond looking for minnows."

Like his brother, Gerald was a student of practical psychology. The "causal observer" saw Gerald "as a fat man with unusually large arms and dark, gray-streaked hair." But he could get inside people's heads. His "fierce black eyes" were "hypnotic."[202]

People talked about Gerald. And his Zoe. She was big, like he was, stayed inside all the time, and never wore anything but a kimono. Plute and Zoe were at an angle to the world. But their eccentricity did not diminish the shimmer of the Ed's badge. Once again, McTeer seemed invulnerable.

Chapter 46

No one ran against Ed McTeer in 1958. It was the start of his eighth term. With his sight back, he was still the law itself, the spoken word. He jokingly told the AP that he had "finally passed his probationary period." He explained how his job had changed: "Today the radio, telephone and airplane made it much more difficult for a fugitive to lose himself in the marshy swamp." A picture ran with the story: Ed in a ten-gallon hat and a light suit with a western cut. He looked dignified, but also a bit flashy. He stood beside his sleek black car, an image of the state of South Carolina emblazoned the door. It could have been a movie poster.[203]

Of course, there would always be outlaws. Moonshine remained among the most prevalent crimes. Five otherwise respectable black men were running a still behind Wiggins general store on St. Helena. Most of the men lived on Lady's Island. Data Jenkins and John Davis lived on St. Helena and took care of it for them. One crisp Sunday afternoon early in 1959, Jenkins and Davis were out tending the still. Shadows and light played across the earth around them. They got to drinking. Jenkins started "raising sand," according to Davis. The men came to blows and Data Jenkins ended up in the fire beneath the still. Davis threw a wet burlap sack over Jenkins' burning back and pulled him from the flames. He didn't know what to do. He went to find the boss, Joe Anderson, leaving Data Jenkins' charred body at the still.

Davis drove to Lady's Island, but Anderson wasn't home. Davis left a message and returned to his own house. At about 10:00 that night, Anderson showed up at Davis's door with a partner. Davis told them what happened. They drove out to the still. Data Jenkins lay there off to the side, battered and burnt, dead.

They wrapped fertilizer sacks around the body and loaded it into a vehicle. They took him out to the lonesomest road they could think of. It took a while. Way too long. Six eyes darted around in the dark like pinballs. They finally found a good spot. And started a fire in the grass. A small orange glow in infinite dark. Enough to blacken the ground. They rolled the body out of the sacks and dumped it onto the fire.

Two kids saw it when they were walking home from school the next day. The kids ran away crying and told their parents, who called the sheriff. McTeer and a deputy arrived at the scene, which was made to look like Jenkins got drunk and fell into his own fire at a makeshift camp. But it didn't look right. The burnt corpse had a broken nose and two contusions on the head.

McTeer learned that Jenkins had worked at a nearby still. There, he found Jenkins' wallet. By the end of the day, he knew who owned the still and where they lived. The deputies spent all day on Lady's Island rounding them up. McTeer questioned Anderson and the others. "In questioning a suspect, I made him know I was looking into his mind. If he told the truth I would know, and if he lied, I would stop him." All five owners gave up Davis—the idiot had ruined the whole thing. John Davis was charged with the murder of Data Jenkins. The others faced accessory after the fact charges in the case that the paper took to calling the "Human Torch."[204]

In addition to the Human Torch case, McTeer investigated the "Ice-pick Killing," a cattle rustling ring and sixty-four other cases that March. In one case, a man named Frank Grant hid outside the bedroom window of his house on Coosaw Island, where cranes were digging up canals for new waterfront lots. Grant watched his wife sleeping inside with their two children. He leveled his rifle and shot her. The blast hit her arm and shattered the bone. Grant rushed the house, busted in, and held eight family members hostage. Somebody managed to slip out a window and called the sheriff. Deputies arrived on the scene, and captured Grant. They took him to jail and his wife to the hospital.[205]

It was not long before Grant was released on bail. He drove over to the water and hid his car in some bushes. He found a skiff, which he took across to Coosaw. He hid the skiff, grabbed his double-barrel shotgun, and again approached the house. When his wife saw him she slammed the door and locked herself in the back room. He splintered the door's cheap wood with an axe. He fired at her, the blast nearly severing her arm at the shoulder where it hit. She screamed; he shot again. The blast struck the cast on her left arm, sending a spray of blood onto the floors and the wall. Grant loaded two more shells. She was still screaming. He shot a third time and blew a hole in the floor, missing her altogether. When the gun jammed, he ran into the kitchen and looked around. People had been talking about the "ice pick killer," so he grabbed the wooden handle. He returned to the room where his wife lay sobbing on the floor in a pool of blood and stabbed her six times with the pick.

The *Gazette* reported that "Grant fled to the marsh, stopping along the way to terrorize students at the island Negro school. Sheriff McTeer said the fugitive covered himself with reeds." McTeer and his men waited until the tide came up and forced him out. The deputies caught and handcuffed him when he scrambled up, soaked and shivering. McTeer was in touch with Solicitor Murdaugh and with the hospital where the wife was taken. If the woman died, he would charge Grant with murder. When she survived, McTeer still pressed for the harshest possible penalty.[206]

Ed knew that every case was unique. But he couldn't help but feel he'd seen it all before. And sometimes, ghosts really did return. A couple of weeks after the Coosaw case, they got a call that an elderly black man was beating his son-in-law. Ed sent a couple deputies out to Port Royal to check it out. When they got there, they arrested the man, who said his name was Brown. They brought him in and had him arraigned by the magistrate, McTeer's former opponent, N.M. Polk. Polk planned to give the man a choice: a hundred bucks or thirty days.

McTeer stopped Polk. He'd heard rumors about Brown. People said he'd killed a man, so they held him. McTeer and Michael went in. The *Gazette* reported that "under intense questioning," Brown admitted that he was not "Brown" at all. His name was Arthur Sushum and he killed a man named Garvin back in 1918 "after the latter took out a warrant against him for stealing chickens." Sushum claimed that he fired after Garvin "pulled a pistol on him when the two met in the road" on the way to the constable.[207]

The forty year-old case was one of the last cold murder cases on the books, but it reminded McTeer of the first murder he ever dealt with back in 1926, when a white man and a black man killed each other on the road for no good reason. If weird lights and eldritch death rattles came with every senseless killing, the county would be awash with the weird, every dog huddled up around its master's legs, afraid to move.

Since human nature had remained the same, there were few motives, but the methods were always changing on both sides of the law.

In July, McTeer hired a former Marine sharpshooter named DeBruhl—recently of the Highway Patrol—to run the night shift. DeBruhl was a different breed of man than Cooler, Koth and Michael. He was big like them, but he walked around with a huge .357 hanging from his hips. He made it known that he was ready to use it. He'd been in several shootouts before. He never lost one. He was a sign of the way things would be.

Chapter 47

Hurricane Gracie hit Coffin Point on 29 September 1959. Ed McTeer called its force "incomprehensible" and compared it to the atomic bomb.

Ed stayed in his car throughout the storm to maintain radio contact with Deputy Michael and the mainland. The family, including a grandchild, remained in the house. Ed told them to move from room to room as the storm hit. He said, "Lucille was calm as a daisy," but admitted she would probably wait out the next storm in town, given what happened next.

Gracie's first gust hit the house hard. Lucille led the family in fleeing to the "nearby plantation superintendent's house when the huge Coffin Point chimneys succumbed to the wind and rain and fell through the roof."

McTeer kept broadcasting from the branch-battered car. Blind gusts of water slammed against the windshield. "Here it comes," Ed told Michael as a "wall of fog" approached. When it reached him, the storm was gone. The sun shone on the dripping world ripped apart. McTeer jumped out of the car. He looked up. There it was, "the Navy hurricane hunter aircraft circling slowly at forty thousand feet."

As "the sunlight and calm began to seem permanent, McTeer said neighbors John Behran and Mrs. VanDerlind came out from their houses."

Ed hollered at them: "We're in the direct eye of the storm. Stay with me or get back in your houses." VanDerlind stayed with the sheriff, and Behran went inside.[208]

Thomas McTeer remembers everybody frantically moving whatever they could from the Big House to the superintendent's house during the calm. He said they got everything but the piano.

On the other side of the eye wall, the air went crazy again and, inflated with fury, it hit at one hundred and forty miles an hour. Ed told the paper "There is no warning increase of wind in such cases. It just hits you full force." It blew in the doors and windows. Wood ripped. Trees fell.

The storm finally passed. McTeer's house was damaged but his family was safe. "Hurricanes can't scare me at all," he told the *Post and Courier.* "But I am frightened for other people." He got back in the car and went to work.

O.C. Michael called Beaufort "a total wreck."[209] At least one St. Helena man was killed by flying debris. Thousands of homes were damaged, dozens of shrimp boats sunk. Many spent weeks without electricity.

With peace restored, Ed drove around to inspect his own properties. When he finally got out to Coosaw Island, he saw how bad it was. His canals had not been able to resist the hurricane. Some people estimate that Gracie reduced the size of the island was reduced by one-third.

Gracie caused over four million dollars of property damage. Knowing that calamity can be the creation of money, McTeer and Keyserling opened an insurance agency with John Woods, McTeer's son-in-law.

Chapter 48

A couple months after the storm, Gerald McTeer died in the Beaufort Naval Hospital. Ed wrote that Plute conquered alcohol "in later years, but not without the help of family and friends. . . Everybody loved and respected him" by the time he died.[210]

Ed would watch out for the widow Zoe the best he could. They held the funeral at her house by the jail that Friday. Deputies Grantham, Bessinger, Griffin, and Rentz were pallbearers along with the police chief and a State Highway Patrol Corporal named L.W. Wallace.

Ed wrote a final paragraph about his brother, a eulogy of sorts. "Plute has passed on, but even today when someone shows his behind, you can hear people say, 'He should've known Plute.' I knew him quite well. . . He was my brother, Gerald McTeer."[211]

The world rolls over a dead man like the ocean over a hole dug on the beach, smoothing out the lost sand, leaving only the spectral trace to be seen by those with second sight or memory.

Worlds ended every day; it was Ed's job to limit the violence involved. McTeer relished the utter strangeness of the past and the limits of human experience. When he and Lucille moved back into the big house, Chlotilde Martin, a reporter and columnist for the *Post and Courier*, and coroner Roger Pinckney's mother-in-law, wrote that "evidence of Ed's collector's fever are to be seen in the den which he has fitted up for himself in the basement."

She described the "helm indicator from the Maine" and noted that "a prize autographed photograph of General John J. Pershing hangs over the mantle piece and there are a number of interesting old books."

His grandchildren remember riding on stuffed animals friends had brought him from safaris in Africa, as he clacked away at the typewriter in his office. They remember peeling the oyster shells from the tabby walls and rows of cans in the bomb shelter room.

Chapter 49

After Gracie, Ed could see the possibility of atomic devastation more clearly. The hurricane helped McTeer imagine the fallout of an increasingly likely Russian attack on the nearby bases. Dread was building like a storm over the ocean. The world was in flux. He would meet what came.

The county McTeer once knew was gone and, along with it, the brand of law enforcement he practiced. Men like DeBruhl, with .357s strapped to their hips, were the future. McTeer was as much an anomaly now as he had been in the early days when the old-timers called him "sheriff without a gun."

Even the root doctors were using guns. Dr. Eagle lived in the Donaldson apartments at the corner of Congress and Boundary, between the bus station and the National Cemetery. Dr. Eagle was also known as P.H. Washington, but people called him Judge. And Judge called everybody "Darlin.'" He claimed he got his "doctor" mantle in 1923 when "a holy man took me across the sea. We visited the Holy Land, the Red Sea, and the Pyramids. He showed me all the mysteries so that I could help people when I got back. We collected incense, tokens, and magic money. Then the holy man said 'You are Dr. Eagle, King of the Birds!'"[212] The King of the Birds liked jewelry and he kept a trunk of money around. More than one person had seen him twirl a pistol, saying: "No nigger going to steal my money."

Valerie Boles, Washington's common-law wife, and later Minerva in *Midnight in the Garden of Good and Evil*, went out to a dance at Lady's Island one cold Friday night, while Washington stayed at home. When dayclean came, she still wasn't home. Finally he heard a car pull up and went down to the parking lot, where he found his wife and another woman stumbling out of Charley Jenkins's cab. Jenkins was still sitting in the cab, when Washington pulled out a .32-20 Smith and Wesson and began firing. Jenkins reached for his .38 automatic and let off nine rounds. "Washington was hit three times in the right arm, once in the left arm and was grazed on the nose." Despite a right arm "shattered by the hail of bullets," Washington managed to get off several more shots, hitting Jenkins "in the left side with a bullet that lodged under the heart next to the lung," *The Gazette* reported. "Another slug struck Jenkins in the face and emerged at the back of his head." Washington got off one more shot, but it struck the car door. "After the battle," the *Gazette* concluded, "Jenkins drove away in his cab and reached the area of Monson and Green streets before he ran the car into a fence and fainted."[213]

Both men were arrested. The court determined that Washington was at fault. Charlie Jenkins was found not guilty of assault and battery with intent to kill. P.H. Washington pleaded guilty to assault and battery of a high and aggravated nature. As a root doctor, Washington had helped McTeer on several cases. The judge offered him a choice: six months or a three hundred dollar fine.

Washington paid the fine, probably in crumpled bills from a battered old trunk.

Chapter 50

On the day Dr. Eagle was convicted, Ed McTeer was appointed to the new Forfeited Land Commission. The Commission announced that the sheriff would auction off nineteen parcels of land in Beaufort, Lady's Island, and St. Helena Island.

Beaufort's population had doubled during McTeer's tenure as sheriff. Twenty-five percent of the growth had come since 1950. By 1960, the white population was over eight times as great as it had been in 1930, while the black population had been cut in half.

The growth was good for Ed's real estate business, but bad for his political career. His vision of the future had been born out. More bridges were built. Northerners moved South to escape "asphalt jungles" and cold winters. This influx of white northerners did little to advance the cause of the county's black population.

Much of McTeer's support had come from the black community. Blacks were allowed to vote in the primaries, but by now they were vastly outnumbered. Ed walked a tough line. He had a reputation of being fair to black people. But he also had a reputation for controlling them. He claimed he always tried to "search for truth so that justice for all people was the rule and not the exception."[214] As civil rights became a prominent national issue once again, his claim would be put to the test. McTeer's fine line would become increasingly difficult to walk.

Cleaver Johnson, the head of the county NAACP in the 1950s and 1960s, considered McTeer an ally. He credited the sheriff with keeping the Klan out of Beaufort. But the greatest civil rights abuse faced by black people in the Sea Islands was the loss of the land they'd owned since the 1862 Port Royal Experiment. As the land was developed it became more valuable, increasing property taxes. The Gullah could not pay the taxes and lost the land.

By the time the Forfeited Land Commission auctioned the first nineteen properties, they had repossessed seventy more. McTeer was responsible for the auctions. Harry Chakides, the owner of Harry's Restaurant, where Ed hung out every morning, recalled one of the auctions. McTeer sat there at a long table. A secretary sat on either side to help with the paper work. Harry recalled that "Mr. Mac called out the property. There was this surveyor who knew the property he called. He was bidding against a black man for the piece of property. The black man said to the sheriff, 'Mr. McTeer,' he said. 'This is my home. This is not an extra piece of property,' he says. He asks, 'You gonna take my home from me?'

"And Mr. Mac looked over at the other fellow, 'This is this man's home,' he said. 'You heard him. Do you still want to bid?' The white surveyor said he did. Well, Mr. Mac knew the surveyor was hard of hearing, deaf in one ear. So Mr. Mac turned his back to him and asked the black guy real quiet what his last bid was. The guy says 'twenty-five dollars.'

"Mr. Mac turned his head away from the surveyor and said real quiet, 'I hear twenty five dollars. . . once. . . twice. . . .' *Bam!* He says, *'Sold!'* and the guy got his land back. I was really struck by that," Chakides concluded. "I thought it was incredible."

Not every one was so impressed with McTeer's form of justice. A group was forming that wanted McTeer out of office. They said he'd had his day. He was too busy to be sheriff.

Even McTeer could see that something had to go. He and his partners realized that the insurance company was too much. In 1961, they sold their agency to Peoples, whose president was John Trask. The *Beaufort Gazette* ran a front page story about the deal. "In a joint statement, partners J.E. McTeer, Leroy Keyserling, and John S. Woods said the move was made in the best interest of their clients and to allow the partners to devote their full time and energies to their real estate business."[215]

Chapter 51

There was no insurance against the end of the world. McTeer grew increasingly concerned about the threat of communism and nuclear war. He finished his bomb shelter at Coffin Point and urged others to build them and to store up canned food. He met with legislators. He finally put out a call for special deputies in case of a war. Seventy-five men responded. He called them together for a special meeting on the night of 19 October 1961.

"The sheriff never has been known for making long speeches," Ed began, "unless he is in the Identification Room. We all have a general idea of why we are here tonight and what we are here for," said McTeer. He looked out at the crowd, whose faces were marked by the fear of the destruction of modern civilization.

"We are getting closer and closer to war, or the brink of war," McTeer said.

"No one knows, except a person who has been in actual warfare, what war is." He told them that in war hungry men readily "revert to a state of savagery."

They would not be sworn in that night. McTeer wanted them to go home, talk it over at the kitchen table, and then come back to another meeting the next week. He would not paint a "blood and thunder" picture, but would try to make them see what would be asked of them.

"Beaufort is a county of islands. It is a hard thing to police islands," he said. "Imagine what will happen, because Savannah and Charleston are prime targets. . . . The refugees will pour in. It will be like the locusts that sweep over the land and there won't be a thing left in two days time," he said.

He told the gathered men: "Under Civil Defense, there will be no judges; there will be no courts; and we will be the law. We will administer justice, savage as it may sound, that is true. Judgments will be summary. People who pillage and rape and murder will be handled on the spot."

McTeer told the men if they were called, they had better come. If they chose to be deputized, they would have to "study radiological warfare and radioactive fallout, because after all is said and done we are not going out foolishly just to say we died. We are going to live as long as we can if we have an atom war. . . . We are going to protect ourselves in every way we can because the right to survive is inherent in all of us. WE WILL SURVIVE!" he boomed. "Some of us will do it."

They held the next meeting on Halloween night. The Special Deputies all raised their right hands. The white men repeated an oath in unison. They were sworn in: Deputies of impending doom.

Chapter 52

The county celebrated Ed McTeer's thirty-fifth year as sheriff with a ceremony and dinner. The governor sent a representative and a letter honoring the sheriff. Chief Deputy O.C. Michael presented him with a plaque from all the deputies. Both men smiled as a flash captured the moment. McTeer wore bulky glasses and a dark suit. His head was round with a balding crown, his nose big, his ears long. He still had some muscle and his shoulders were broad, but he looked small, frail, and old beside his muscular deputy wearing a uniform and a flat top. They each rested a hand on the plaque between them.

McTeer could look out at everyone gathered. They were all thinking the same thing. He was old, it was getting time to move on, to settle full-time into the real estate that took most of his time now anyway. He knew that. Even his family wanted him out. Perhaps Lucille most of all.

When he started he was too young. Now he was too old. But he couldn't give it up. Not yet. He wanted to do it his way. He wanted to be sure the right man was in charge.

It was not hard to see that each deputy imagined himself as the next sheriff. Each thought he knew how to improve the office. McTeer couldn't begrudge them that. It was not disloyal. He probably would have felt the same way, if he had ever been anybody's deputy. He had wanted to step down several times, toyed with the idea at least. It was fine in the abstract. But it was hard to imagine another actual man as High Sheriff.

The deputies were good men. McTeer knew each of them well. He thought back to the older deputies he'd lost, Randolph, Koth, Cooler.

He thought of Plute most of all, recalled him as deputy and then jailer. He wanted to protect his family and to keep them close. He made sure repairs were made and everyone was back at Coffin Point before Christmas.

He set up an eight-foot tree that tickled the new ceiling above the long dining room table, and they decked it out. Everyone dressed formally. McTeer sat at the head of the table. Lucille and the girls had been cooking all morning. Ed had probably killed the bird. Thomas was home from military school. Everyone was there. McTeer proposed a toast, with sherry.

Sometime that day, Deputy Grantham died in a car wreck. He had been one of Plute's pallbearers, along with Bessinger and Wallace. Now, the same men helped lay Grantham in the ground. McTeer hired his former opponent N.M. Polk and put him on the night patrol with DeBruhl.

Chapter 53

W.H. Stanley, a farmer from Burton, declared against McTeer in 1962. He paid his fee to enter the primary, filled out the paper work, but later changed his mind, asked for the money back, and withdrew. A short time later, he decided to file again. The committee ruled he was ineligible now. Stanley used the fee money to buy an ad in the *Gazette*. "I have been denied the opportunity of re-entering the sheriff's race in the primary election June 13," wrote Stanley. "I will be a candidate for the office in the general election in November," he declared. "Public Sentiment is demanding a choice of candidates. Beaufort County needs a man for sheriff to devote his full time to the duties, which you the voters have entrusted to him; not one that devotes part-time himself and employs extra deputies at tax-payer expense while he works for private interests."[216]

The paper asked Ed about Stanley's challenge. "I think the things set out by Mr. Stanley are truly worthwhile and am in agreement," Ed replied. "Except with reference to his own qualifications for the position," he added. "As I am reaching the end of my career as sheriff, Mr. Stanley will have a chance in the not-too-distant future to offer himself in the Democratic primary and at that time he can state his qualifications for the sheriff's job." Ed voted for Nixon in 1960, but he still assumed one must be a Democrat—and stand in the primary—to be sheriff of Beaufort County.

"I feel certain that by that time, Mr. Stanley will have had a chance to make up his mind whether or not he desires to run," McTeer said. "I certainly would have no desire to continue my career as sheriff of Beaufort County if Mr. Stanley comes close to winning in the general election on a write-in basis."[217]

Stanley didn't have a chance. But there in Stanley's doomed campaign was the answer McTeer's enemies had been seeking. The sheriff's only objection was Stanley's lack of experience and ability, so they would find an experienced challenger to face him. After all, McTeer had basically admitted that he only devoted part-time to the job. And there was that press release saying that he was getting out of insurance to focus "full-time on real estate."

Deputy Bessinger, one of Plute's pall-bearers, started collecting signatures to run against Ed in the primary. But when Stanley announced as a write-in, Bessinger suddenly said that he would also run as a write-in. Stanley would get a few votes, after all. Maybe he would take them from the sheriff.

Rumors spread across the county like fire ants. Some claimed that L.W. Wallace, another of Plute's pall-bearers, would run. Wallace had been a corporal in the State Highway Patrol in Beaufort for the last fourteen years. The commander of the highway patrol publicly announced Wallace's retirement, just in time for the election. It was a surprise to most people. Perhaps Wallace had been planning to run, but that September he "suffered an illness that required hospitalization." While in the hospital Wallace was asked about "reports that friends were booming him as a write-in candidate for sheriff," but he had no comment and said "he planned to join the staff of the Beaufort Oil Company."

Asked again, he wrote a statement to the press: "I appreciate greatly the interest of my friends in suggesting me as a write-in candidate for sheriff of Beaufort County. However, I must say I am not a write-in candidate and I cannot be a write-in candidate for sheriff." The *Gazette* reported that "he indicated that he if ever ran for sheriff, it would be as a regular party candidate, not a write-in."[218]

On 18 October, just weeks before the election, Bessinger dropped out. He said, "In my business and my campaigning, I have covered most of Beaufort County, and everywhere I went I found that people felt it was time for a change in the sheriff's office and that they would like to vote for Mr. Wallace. So, I am stepping aside as a candidate and would like to ask my friends to join me in supporting Mr. Wallace." The *Gazette* reported: "In Sheriff's Race: Wallace Candidate; Bessinger is Out."

It was the first real sheriff's race since 1926, when McTeer faced Deputy Cooler and W.F. Sanders. It was the first time since Reconstruction the race would be decided in the general election and not the primary.

McTeer responded to Wallace's candidacy: "I have complete confidence in the ability of the people of Beaufort County to select the man they want to serve them as their sheriff. I am willing to abide by the results of the November election."[219]

Wallace was forty one years old. He came from Laurens County in the up-state. One of his daughters had been crowned Miss Beaufort the previous year. She was at USC now and her sister was at the high school. They were prominent in the Baptist church. Dr. Jones, the pastor, was one of the friends who convinced him to run. That was part of the insurgency. The Episcopalians had run the town for so long. Florence McTeer's First-class Pullman to heaven offended the Baptists. They had the numbers, now they wanted the power. These "Whiskey-palians" were blue-blooded degenerates. Ed, they said, screwed anything that moved. And then there was this root doctor stuff.

Lt. Col. Baxley of the 2009 Sheriff's Office was far removed from the 1962 election, but when I first asked him about McTeer, he said, "Me and my wife are good Baptists and Little Ed lent me those scrap books before he took them over to the library. We got to about the second page with that voodoo stuff and I got up and got my keys and locked those books away in the trunk of the patrol car until I could take them back to him. Didn't want anything to do with them. Didn't even want to touch them. Never looked in there again."

Then there were the people for whom race was the issue. Even without the voodoo, he seemed a little too friendly with the blacks. People remembered the property auctions. They recalled that he had kept the Klan out of town. And according to Roger Pinckney people talked about "bribes from Gullah bootleggers."[220]

The claim that he was not a "full-time sheriff" hit McTeer hardest. He was too old. He looked too shabby, not firm enough. The world had changed and it looked bad for the county to have a sheriff who'd been around since prohibition.

McTeer suggested Wallace hold up his qualifications during the Democratic Party primary, participate in the stump speeches, and then give people a chance to decide. Wallace responded with an ad that told voters, "The General Election is the real election, the legal election. Don't let anyone try to deprive you of your rights and privileges of choosing the man you want for sheriff."

"The Loyal Friends and Supporters of Sheriff J.E. McTeer," were worried enough to print a full page ad headlined "We Salute Sheriff J.E. McTeer." The three columns of text began: "During the past three or four decades, vast social, economic, and political changes have taken place in our country and indeed the entire world." Through all of the changes "Beaufort has remained an oasis of peace and tranquility and law and order in the midst of a wasteland of organized crime, 'asphalt jungle,' dope peddling, robbery, rapine, and mob violence." It wasn't an accident they argued: Ed McTeer kept the county safe.

The Loyal Friends claimed that "a vicious and unfounded whisper campaign," was trying to destroy this order. The Loyal Friends added that "an investigation into the initial sources of the vicious rumors" would "reveal that their originators are embittered would-be dictators who, frustrated in their own attempts to dominate the politics of the Beaufort County, now seek political revenge against one who they blame, with good reason, for their downfall."

In order to fight the part-time sheriff attack, McTeer needed to show that his accomplishments weren't all in the distant past. They had just passed through the Cuban Missile Crisis. The ad reminded voters of McTeer's foresight. He had appointed his Civil Defense Deputies a year earlier. A Marine General recently praised him. The message seemed to be: *If the world ends, who do you want to be your sheriff?*

Wallace responded. He bought radio and newspaper ads. He gave pencils to the voters and showed them how to write in his name on the ballot. He urged them not to believe last minute rumors. By Election Day, Wallace had spent $995.26 "principally for radio and newspaper advertising, pencils and travel." W.H. Stanley spent $202.56—but at least he didn't have to pay the entrance fee for the Democratic Party primary. Ed McTeer spent $47.12.

You didn't need ESP to see the race would be close.[221]

"In the evening of the general election day in 1962, early returns gave Wallace the lead," wrote Alexia Jones Helsley, the daughter of Dr. Jones, the Baptist minister and one of Wallace's biggest backers. The first count of votes looked like Wallace would have 2006 votes and McTeer 1967. "Wallace supporters had gathered at his home when a radio broadcast disrupted their celebration. Calhoun Thomas, chairman of the Beaufort County Democratic Party, announced over the radio that another ballot box had been found and the results of the election were in question." It seems that some of the votes for "County" seats had been put in "State" boxes in both Beaufort and St. Helena. Helsley reported that a group of men left Wallace's house. They "hurried to the community center, located on Carteret Street next door to the post office where the ballot boxes were being stored. Amid fears that the election was being 'stolen,' they learned that the Lady's Island results had been phoned in and that the box remained on the island."[222] Jones and his neighbor Elbert Sweat drove out Lady's Island. They secured the ballot box and insisted that it be stored in the vault of the People's Bank. John Trask—whom many called "Boss Trask"—was the president of People's Bank and one of Wallace's primary backers.

The County claimed "neither candidate has asked for a recount but that it would be conducted anyway 'in response to popular demand.'" Ed carried Dale-Lobeco, Burton Landing, Sheldon, and Daufuskie (unanimously). He won big in three high population precincts: Bluffton, Hilton Head, and St. Helena. But he lost even bigger in Burton, Port Royal, and the biggest precinct, Beaufort, where Wallace got 1,071 votes, half of his total. McTeer did better with the old-timers and the African Americans. Wallace was winning among the twenty eight percent of the population that had come since the 1950 census.

Still, Wallace's lead was smaller when the votes were recounted. McTeer was down by twenty-seven votes, 2,006 to 1,979. And Stanley got sixty-seven votes—enough to have flipped the thing. Assistant Attorney General J.C. Coleman reported to the Election Commission that the election had been "properly conducted."[223] That was when all of those irregularities about the "County" and "State" votes got interesting to Ed McTeer and his lawyer, William Levin.

Chapter 54

McTeer filed a petition with the Board challenging the outcome on several grounds. First he argued: "At the various polling precincts in Beaufort County, and particularly in the Beaufort box, a number of ballots for the office of sheriff were found in the box designated and labeled for state offices. That these ballots were withdrawn from the box and commingled and counted with the other regularly cast ballots for county office is in violation of the province of Section 23-358 of South Carolina."

McTeer's petition went on to argue that "several of the larger polling precincts have failed to account for all the ballots cast." He explained that there were "considerable discrepancies between the total of the names of the voters appearing on the polling list and the total vote as presently tabulated." Further, the "ballots at the Beaufort box were not counted separately by the managers, as required by law, but were assembled in batches by others and their count accepted as true count without certification." Finally, McTeer pointed out that many polling places had only counted the ballots where a voter had actually checked McTeer's name. He argued that a voter unaware of Mr. Wallace's write-in campaign would have no reason to check the name of a candidate in an uncontested race—especially if he was a straight Democratic ticket voter.[224]

The Board of Canvassers deliberated over the case for twelve hours. They agreed to a hearing that would include both candidates and their lawyers.

At the hearing, Mr. Levin questioned the legitimacy of the "illegally cast ballots." Such ballots should not be counted. He brought to the stand a Mr. Julius Levin (apparently of no relation), a poll-worker in Beaufort.

The witness said, "I was at the table when the state box was opened. Mr. W.F. Scheper opened the state box and turned the box upside down and dropped the ballots on the table. At that time he found quite a few County ballots in the State box. I told Mr. Scheper that the law provided that . . . where the ballots were placed in the wrong box they should not be counted. He then put those ballots aside." A few moments later another manager named Felix Greene, who was also Secretary of the Democratic Party, came over and took the ballots and "commingled" them with the others. Levin said they later found more irregular votes. He testified that there were a minimum of forty and a maximum of sixty. Enough to put the outcome in question, even though Greene testified "that is the way we have been doing it in Beaufort County."[225]

The Board of Canvassers declared the election "Null and Void" and asked Governor Fritz Hollings to call a new election.

There were still a lot of questions. When would the election be held? Would Wallace's name be on the ballot? Or would he be a write-in again? Was it legal for the Board of Canvassers to certify elections selectively? Had they, in effect, called into question all of Beaufort's votes in every race? Would the entire election be conducted again?

The only thing they knew was that there would be another election and so the campaign continued, unabated. Before a date was set, Wallace ran a prominent ad that laid out the events of the past weeks. He attributed all the confusion to McTeer's machinations and dirty tricks: "At this time I do not know when the election will be, nor what kind of tactics may be used to persuade you to change your mind. All I can say is that I humbly appreciate the manner in which you have rallied to my side to assure you that I shall continue to stand ready to discuss with any of you such accusations as may be brought against me." He concluded the ad, "Once already, you have clearly expressed your preference. Ordinarily, once is enough but in this case, it appears that you must repeat yourself in a real loud voice so that everybody—even losers—will understand."

Governor Hollings called for a new election on 11 December. Wallace argued that his name should be printed on the ballot. The Attorney

General informed him and the County Board that "the instructions to voters would be the same on December 11 as it had been on November 6, even though only one name would appear on the ballot." It was also decided that the alleged irregularities had affected only the sheriff's race. No other positions would be involved in the new election. The other races were beyond suspicion.[226]

McTeer and his lawyer argued that there should not be a new election at all. A majority of voters had taken a loyalty oath to the Democratic Party when they voted in the primary. They were violating that oath if they voted for Wallace. Wallace responded with an ad that asked *What About That Oath?* and reminded voters: "You are free American citizens, and still have the right to vote as you please." He went on to address McTeer's claims directly.

"Not only has the Supreme Court declared the primary oath to be meaningless and unconstitutional, but at the time of the primary, the incumbent was nominated without opposition, so his name did not actually appear on the ballot." Wallace reminded voters that McTeer had said he was "willing to abide by the results of the November election."

Wallace promised that he would be a "full-time sheriff without business interests to consume my time." He promised that "sheriff's department automobiles and other equipment [would] be used only for official business." He promised to have "at the jail a full-time, competent, paid turn-key, qualified to handle such matters as may be brought to his attention" and improve "conditions at the jail." He promised to ensure that "persons calling the sheriff's office any hour of the day or night, will reach either me or a competent representative of the department."

McTeer reminded voters that Wallace told the *Gazette*: "I must say that I am not a write in candidate and I cannot be a write-in candidate for sheriff."

McTeer said he "challenged his opponent and his opponent's principle backer to public debate. Offer has not been accepted, to date." He called himself the "Independent Candidate" who is "neither backed nor owes any political obligations to any embittered or dispossessed political groups or individuals who want to make Beaufort a 'Wide open' County." He concluded his qualifications, pointing out his "outstanding physical and mental endurance during periods of stress."

New rumors spread and dominated the campaign. People said Wallace "molested" the wife of a doctor on the doctor's desk while he was away deer hunting. Roger Pinckney wrote that "the charges and countercharges finally attracted so much attention that a Charleston television station agreed to a debate of sorts." Even so, "they were afraid to have the armed antagonists face each other before the cameras," so instead "each would read a half hour long campaign speech over the air." According to Pinckney, Ed McTeer cited his experience, and his respect for the community, black and white alike. But the following evening," Pinckney reported, "when the challenger's response was to be aired, television screens all over the Lowcountry dissolved into a flutter, buzz, and blur of interference."[227]

Otherwise, things were not going well for McTeer. It sometimes seemed as if it had been hopeless from the start. The very act of questioning the previous results seemed to prove Wallace's points about the abuses of power in McTeer's office. In a final ad, McTeer wrote about his accomplishments: "No Gambling. No Bootlegging. No Prostitution Over the Counter or UNDER it." He added that "Things have gone so clean and happy for so long that we never pause to ask ourselves why this is true in our county nor to give credit where credit is due. If a man can't stand on his record where and how is he to stand?"

He concluded with a lamentation. "It must be discouraging indeed for anyone seeking public office to be confronted with the possibility that no matter what his integrity, his conscientious pursuit of his obligation of office, he may in the end, after years of forthright, upright service to the community which he has served, be tossed aside without appreciation of the past or thought of the future.

"If it is change that is wanted, why not take it to the lawmakers, the legislators. Our sheriff's duty is simply to carry out the laws which we ourselves make."

During the last week, the *Gazette* reported that "flanked by their sharply divided supporters, the two candidates for sheriff of Beaufort County this week stepped up the pace of their aggressive campaigns, to be culminated, next Tuesday, when the voters converge on the polls for an historic 'second' election."[228]

When the day finally arrived, "the two opponents, generally bulwarked by members of their families, doggedly held their positions at the Beaufort Community Club, the county's largest poll, throughout the bitingly cold day to great the voters as they made their appearance." It must have been clear to Ed early on. "Pencil wielding voters to write in the name of L.W. Wallace" were flooding the polls. But Beaufort had gone to Wallace heavy in the first race as well. Maybe the islands would come through for McTeer.

The *Gazette* reported, "despite the unpleasant weather throughout the day, they marched into the booths in even larger numbers than they did on November 6 when there were several heated contests to claim their attention."[229]

There would be no state box to confuse things this time, somebody joked. When the polls closed at 6:00, McTeer went back to his office at the County Courthouse to wait for the returns. The marsh and the river and the bay across Bay Street from the art deco Court House were flecked with the glinting hardness of steel mist as evening fell on the day of the second election. There'd been some reports of irregularities on Hilton Head, where Ed was winning. This looked bad, since he was down everywhere else. The worst was St. Helena, his home for over a decade now. He had won by nearly two hundred votes in the first race; now he was down by a hundred. McTeer must have wondered, what had happened to make 289 people change their mind about him.

McTeer carried Bluffton, Hilton Head and Daufuskie. But even on Daufuskie three of the sixteen voters defected to Wallace. By 7:30, it was all done. Wallace had carried eight precincts, twice as many as in the first election.

Wallace, "a tired but elated man, said, 'I will ever be grateful and obligated to the people of Beaufort County.'" The *Gazette* added that Wallace "pledged his best efforts as sheriff as his means of showing appreciation."

McTeer got the returns in his office. The night was dark. The cold seeped in. He got in his car and drove the twenty minutes to Coffin Point, watching as the hood of the car ate the road in front of him.

Once home, he picked up the phone and dialed the *Gazette*. He said: "I congratulate Mr. Wallace and I am glad that it is over."[230]

McTeer ran a short ad in the paper that read: "To the Citizens of Beaufort County: I wish to thank the people for their support during my long tenure in office. I wish for Mr. Wallace the best of luck."

Wallace's was longer. "To the People of Beaufort County," it read. "I would like to take this means of expressing my heartfelt support for the generous manner in which you supported me, thus making it possible for me to serve as your county sheriff. At this happy season of the year, I would like to wish each of you a Joyous Christmas and to invite your continued support and cooperation as we move together into the New Year. L.W. Wallace."

Many of McTeer's deputies lost their positions. DeBruhl took Michael's place as chief deputy. John Trask gave a valuable piece of waterfront land with a fishing camp to Sheriff Wallace's office.

Cleaver Johnson was the head of the NAACP in Beaufort when McTeer lost. He recalled seeing McTeer not long after the election. "He didn't want to lose that sheriff. He didn't want to lose that. He was hurted. He was hurted. And a lot of black and a lot of whites were hurted too cause McTeer was such a good man."

Chapter 55

McTeer suddenly had time to wonder what caused the election to go so poorly. He fell back into the obscurity of private life. It was a questionable luxury he had not indulged since youth. Certainly, both he and Lucille welcomed the "absence of the incessant ringing of the telephone at all hours of the night."[231] But he still had that sheriff's blood. He once told the press "I was not born to live a sedentary life. An overabundance of nervous energy has made me to create adventure where there was none."[232] But the press did not come around and call anymore. McTeer must have recalled his father's loss to Sheriff White so may years ago. God, how long had it been? Fifty years now, almost exactly.

He'd learned the root from White, and then from Emmaline and Tony Legare when they had been forced to move to the farm out in Grays Hill, where he and Plute and the girls had grown up, where Langford had been murdered. Oh, he could remember it all so well.

McTeer retired as a root doctor when he lost the sheriff's position. Perhaps it really had been a means to control the black population, as many of the white people thought. Anyway nobody came to him with their problems anymore. It was like he was just out of high school again, trying to figure out what to do with his life. His father and White had both died in office. What can you do after you are sheriff? He later wrote of the Great Retirement:

> Lord, I've lead a busy life
> And at the end of my road
> I'd be embarrassed if you found me
> Waiting my turn at shuffleboard!

Like his father before him, Ed would have to find other ways to satisfy that sheriff's blood. He continued to work in real estate. Hunting and fishing kept him outdoors and so he prayed,

> Let me go with the roar of surf in my ears;
> And a fish running strong on the line.
> Here I've shed my cares throughout the years
> With the passing of my time.[233]

Ed McTeer III recalls his father "standing in the surf in his underwear, surf fishing with a straw hat on." He had fifteen grandchildren by this time and Georgiana's daughter, Betsy Cooke, recalled, "He taught me to surf fish. He taught me to fish from a boat. He even got tickled when I got the bigger fish. He wore my grandmother's bright red lipstick when he went fishing cause there wasn't any sunscreen."

He kept the real estate office on West Street. He drove to town every morning and met his old pals at Harry's Restaurant. It was the same group who always met there at the table they called the "Booth of Knowledge." Every day was the same. They had a word for the day and they would work that word into all their discussions or use it to start new ones. They investigated serious problems. Harry recalls the time they spent trying to riddle out how a fly landed on a ceiling, upside down. One of the guys had a son up at NASA who typed up their discussion and sent it to a friend and had a report sent back with equations and diagrams. There was always something new to discuss. They were old men and the world was changing quickly. The faces changed too. McTeer wrote his best poem "The Vacant Chair," about it:

> It's an old Beaufort custom
> To assemble every day
> And discuss the world's condition
> At Harry's on the Bay.

But Ed noticed that things had changed, even at Harry's, since he'd retired.

Now when I drop a pearl of wisdom
Much to my surprise
No one argues with me
They just avert their eyes.
No longer comes the greeting
'How are you feeling Ed?'
I know I'm a Senior Citizen
For it's 'Mr. Mac' instead.[234]

The poem recalled when he was first invited by the town elders to sit around the table, upon his return from Baltimore. One by one he had watched those old men slip away. Younger faces had replaced them. He knew that one day before too long there would be another empty chair at the table, another young man asked to join the group.

He was not in the underworld yet, but time had become crepuscular, filled with long-flickering shadows. Now he could only watch the world he once made. It happened just as his longtime concerns, race and magic, moved into the center of culture.

Chapter 56

In 1963, Dr. Martin Luther King, Jr. came to the Penn Center in Frogmore, out towards Lands End, only miles from Coffin Point. The Penn School was created as part of the Port Royal Experiment in 1862. Now a Quaker couple, the Siceloffs, ran the Penn Center on its campus. It was one of the few places in the South willing to host interracial meetings. The Southern Christian Leadership Conference (SCLC) came to the Center to plan the March on Washington. There was some hostility and local white opposition to the meeting, despite attempts to keep it secret. "Sometimes it seemed the people in Beaufort knew the SCLC was coming" before the Center's staff did, a 1997 article in the *Friends Journal* reported.[235] A 2008 *New York Times* article quoted Joseph Dominick, a former staff member of the Penn Center saying, "We couldn't notify any law enforcement people because we didn't know who would be in that little group that would be after doing him in, see what I mean?"[236]

Cleaver Johnson of the NAACP agreed it wasn't safe to tell Wallace about King's visit. Was he a racist?

"Well, if he wasn't a racist, he act that way. Yeah, yeah they had the Klan rally. Klan would rally and they start off like a church service and somebody pray and then after that, little bitty man, the head dragon they called him. . . I didn't see in the paper or nothing but they say McTeer tell Wallace not to let them people come in here. I didn't hear it myself. You know, somebody say McTeer told him not to do it, stop them from coming."

When the Klan did come, Mr. Siceloff "called the sheriff because he had heard rumors that after the rally the Klan would come to the Center. The sheriff told the Siceloffs to write down the license numbers of the Klan cars when they saw them." He told them the department would be patrolling the area in unmarked cars. The Siceloffs noted with relief that there were more deputies than Klansmen at the Center that day.

King returned to the center often between 1963 and 1967. He stayed in the small, primitive Gant Cabin where some people think he wrote parts of the iconic "I Have a Dream" speech. The Center began to build a special cabin for King, a "retreat within a retreat," as the *New York Times* put it. But Martin Luther King was assassinated in Memphis before he ever used the cabin. The world blew up. McTeer's worst fears had entered the subconscious of the nation and exploded in the cities with a crazy dream logic. McTeer watched on TV as the flames engulfed D.C., Baltimore, Detroit. There were no riots in Beaufort, but the First Union African Baptist Church on Daufuskie quit ringing its bell. It would not ring again for decades.

McTeer's experience seemed relevant. But he was old. The younger generations did not care what he thought about the present. They were eager for his stories of the past, but they did not see the connection.

McTeer recalled a common scene in the years after his retirement. People would say to him: "You've been the court of domestic relations, juvenile court, and Beaufort's father confessor for years. You should write a book like *Peyton Place*."

"If I did," Ed would reply, "we would have to widen the bridges and make a four lane highway for the exodus, and I guess I'd be traveling with the crowd."[237]

But he had a hell of a title: *High Sheriff of the Low Country*. And he had stories, things that should be remembered, so he wrote the book, clacking away on his typewriter in his room full of old artifacts, burning black lines into the edge of his desk with the endless stream of cigarettes that yellowed the tabby walls like age itself.

Chapter 57

The book was a sort of magic that took him back and let him recall what the world he had known felt like before it was gone. He remembered when it was hard to get to Hilton Head; now they were putting men on the moon. While he was writing the book things continued to go crazy: race riots, the Black Panthers, the Klan, Malcolm X, the war, the anti-war students, dope, and the occult.

They world had felt the sway of imminent doom in October 1962, engulfed by the feeling that the world could end atomically, and this was the fallout. Ed recalled when they first started talking about the hydrogen bomb and the speech he gave that chilly night, the longest in his career. He could still see the fear in the faces of the men he deputized in the face of destruction. Now people were responding to annihilation with nihilism. McTeer sat at his desk and wrote: "Cults and mysticism are the in thing today all across the nation. Californians especially have more than revived the old spirit of occultism and witchcraft. . . . Movies such as *Rosemary's Baby* and ritual murders involving entertainment personalities all serve to promote and perpetuate this ancient art. Black magic is rapidly becoming a synonym for big money and more and more people are trying to get on the bandwagon."[238]

In California, Tex Watson and other members of the Manson Family entered the home of *Rosemary's Baby* director Roman Polanski and his pregnant wife Sharon Tate. Polanski was filming overseas. Watson declared, "I am the devil and I'm here to do the devil's business." He and his companions killed five people. They took the blood of the victims and wrote on the walls, hoping to encourage a race war.

Five days later, Ed McTeer had to go to the Dowling, Dowling, Sanders and Dukes Law Firm. It was 14 August 1969. When he walked into the office, he saw Dr. Eagle and his wife Valerie. The waiting room was full but McTeer made his way over to his old colleague. The two old men, one white, one black, sat together in a public place a year after the King riots to discuss witchcraft five days after the Manson murders.

McTeer noticed how much Washington had aged since they'd last met. He described Dr. Eagle as a "gaunt old man." His goatee was graying. But his fingers were still studded with flashy gold rings. Each one symbolized his familiarity with a particular spirit. These rings worked with the purple glasses to "let the disappointed, unhappy, sick, and unjustly used of the county recognize him as a man who could help."

They forgot the bustle of the room and focused on the future of the root. McTeer was anxious for news. He explained that he had retired from rootwork.

"I know you only work the sickness and death roots now that you're out of the business," Dr. Eagle said. Then he complained, "When you did work you always put Dr. Buzzard and Dr. Bug ahead of me. You don't know they sent to me for their high priced roots."

McTeer: "You just say that now because they're both dead and now you are king."

They talked about the old days. Dr. Eagle recalled how all three doctors had tried to put the court powder on the sheriff. It didn't work. They'd never had trouble with court roots before. The doctors came together, Washington told McTeer, and decided to work with him.

The old men enjoyed the renewal of their acquaintance. "I'm getting old," Dr. Eagle declared just as Dr. Buzzard had two decades earlier. "Things have changed from the old days. I have to talk with you. I have questions to ask and treasures to show you."

Dr. Eagle invited McTeer to come to his place on Congress Street before he and Valerie left the office. The white secretaries were listening in, and they asked McTeer if he was really going to go. He said he couldn't wait to see the changes and advances in the science of rootwork.

The next morning McTeer pulled into the same parking lot where Washington had the shoot out with the cabdriver years earlier. McTeer went to the door and Valerie told him that Dr. Eagle was finishing up with a customer. He sat down and waited. Shortly, the door opened and a white woman walked out. Washington greeted McTeer with a delighted exclamation. He invited McTeer into his room and told Valerie they were not to be disturbed. McTeer called Dr. Eagle's room "the birthplace of Beaufort County's crop of modern roots and potions."

There were shelves lined with jars and barrels of powder. McTeer remarked that business must be good. Dr. Eagle told him that things had changed in the world of rootwork. "We don't go into graveyards anymore and look for special roots and things. We buy straight from a factory in Baltimore now." Of course, he explained, the factory was legitimate; it had direct connections to Egypt and the Orient. He pointed at the shelves, his right arm still slower from the gunshots, his nose still scarred. There was court powder, love powder—sometimes called "Essence of bend-over"—powder for courage, for gambling, and for general good luck.

Dr. Eagle showed McTeer all of this with great pride. "All I have to do is speak over those in an unknown tongue," he bragged. He had a metal detector for finding roots buried in yards. A woman on Johns Island sent him roots to chew in court. But to be honest, Dr. Eagle told McTeer, unless it was a serious case he didn't go to court anymore. It took too long, waiting for the jury to deliberate and all the rising and sitting for the judge and that business. Now he just sold the root to the client and let him chew it his own self.

Washington had presents for McTeer. He offered him two lodestones, perfume from Egypt and a coin from the Holy Land. "How about your sex life?" Dr. Eagle asked, offering "a strong powder for that."

"I make my own powder for that," McTeer replied. But he gladly accepted the other gifts. "For my powers have weakened since I quit practicing," he explained.

Dr. Eagle was happy that the old sheriff received his offerings. He had a big question to ask, something that had been troubling him. He asked McTeer if he believed that men had really landed on the moon. "The moon controls all the spirits of the mind," Dr. Eagle explained. "If they had put foot on that, they would have been wiped out." He believed that the landing had been staged.

The spirits represented by Dr. Eagle's rings were lunar beings. McTeer surmised that the moon landing presented a crisis of faith for Dr. Eagle. McTeer quickly agreed that the moon was a mystic body. He told Washington "they can do all kinds of things with cameras."

Dr. Eagle was visibly relieved. The two men agreed to meet again.[239]

McTeer took this encounter back into the tabby room and wrote about it. A short time later, he returned to Dr. Eagle's with a *National Geographic* photographer named Thomas Nebbia who photographed the two men together. One of the photos ended up as the cover of *High Sheriff of the Low Country*. In the picture, both men wore ties and short-sleeved button-up shirts. They stared through thick glasses at voodoo dolls, like two physicians studying x-rays as the world burned around them.

Dr. Eagle wrote a note giving McTeer "wholehearted permission" to use his name and image in the book. He wrote that he and the sheriff "worked closely together helping people who were under the influence of spells." McTeer signed the document as a witness.[240]

After the encounter, McTeer wrote the "good old days of witchcraft are gone now." He lamented that the root doctor "no longer has the time to take a man to the graveyard to communicate with the dead. . . . This is the day of mass-production, the quick buck and bustle, and the root doctor is keeping pace."[241]

After his meeting with Dr. Eagle, Ed McTeer got the second sight a second time. He knew what to do with his life. He would revive his old practice. There was a new language for it now, and a new need. He could help people with cosmic problems in the astral realm. He could be a "poor man's psychiatrist."

Chapter 58

The book solidified the myth of Dr. Buzzard and the White Prince. The *High Sheriff of the Low Country* prompted the press to call again. This time the stories were different. Ed was the narrator rather than actor; the stories were *about* him. And since he was no longer running for office, they were never critical. Nearly every one of them ran a big picture of the old sheriff with a voodoo doll. He told about the rum-runners and the murders, but people really wanted to hear about witchcraft. He gave lectures and interviews.

The year after the *High Sheriff of the Low Country,* Ed McTeer published *Beaufort Now and Then*. The first half of the book, "The Early Days," recounts the history of Beaufort county leading up to the twentieth century. It is not a scholarly history, but rather the sweeping story of an island county told by an old raconteur, a flood of grand tales and startling facts. It expressed a love of time as much as a love of place.

In the second part, "The Beaufort I Knew," Ed McTeer wrote about his father, mother, sisters, and Old Plute; he wrote about the Indian Gang, the bath houses, and Lizzie's Place. As he remembered all the people he'd known and loved, he watched them move like ghosts around the tabby-walled room where he worked. If he could capture something of the wild world he had known and make it visible again, that would be real magic. If he could talk to old Plute again, listen to him for just an instant. . . He could hear him at the Yacht Club, "It's a lie! It's a malicious lie! He must be blind! Why anyone can see you only have two chins." Ed decided to end the book with the chapter about Gerald.

The book mentioned witchcraft only once. McTeer wrote that he beat his opponents because the voters were afraid: "If I found out they had not voted 'right' I might even have brought to my aid Dr. Buzzard and Dr.

Eagle who are my cohorts." The elections had gotten all mixed up in his mind—he seemed to mix details from 1928 and 1938—but it was rootwork that everybody asked about anyway.

And it wasn't just the press who was asking. "Everybody knows I'm retired as a witchdoctor," he told a reporter in 1971. "But I still get calls by the dozen from all over the United States."[242] He wouldn't travel, but he didn't turn anyone away. He would see them, as long as they came to him. He did not accept money. He told them, just as he had in the old days, that the root would turn on them both if he accepted payment. He suggested charities to those who felt the need to give.

Ed reported that Lucille came to know many of the callers. Someone asked her if she was afraid of her witchdoctor husband. "Afraid? I should say not. I know all of his secrets. If he tries anything funny with me, I'll just put a root on him he won't forget."[243]

He did not practice full time. He continued to dabble in real estate. He came out with a third book the next year, *Adventure in the Woods and Waters of the Low Country*. He did not mention witchcraft or rootwork at all. He dedicated the first book to Lucille, the second to his children, and this book to Clifford Baxter, his hunting buddy for many decades. They were both getting too old to do much hunting, now, and McTeer took real joy in reliving his former exploits. The book was like the collection of animal heads hanging on the wall of his downstairs room, a collection of trophy stories, wild shadows of the crazy things that happen over a lifetime in the creeks and the woods and the sea. He often remarked "anything abnormal in the human or animal kingdom quickly draws my interest."[244]

The stories in *Adventure* were about the relationship between the human and animal kingdoms. He recalled the old days at the hunting clubs of the wealthy, the Guggenheims and Vanderbilts and all the others. He remembered the constant competition. He and Baxter were one pair and Brantley Harvey and Mr. Stock another. Year after year they vied for bragging rights among duck hunters. As he recalled, no one else was even in the game. He remembered his old friend Mattie Simmons who'd "been born in the wrong era . . . who could not survive if adventure and danger were not around." The words were a mirror in which he could see himself reflected.

He had always needed the excitement and the danger. Even on his rare day off from patrolling the county he had been out on the sea or in a swamp somewhere on a deer stand or a duck blind. He had been unable to sit still. Now he could no longer act, but he would recall it all, remember it, so that something would live of the actions that fall forgotten with the dead. It was time to assess his life. For he was getting old.

McTeer's poems were interspersed through the volume. In "Metamorphosis," he noted that

> I never felt better
> Last night when I went to bed
> But when I woke this morning
> I found my youth had fled.

At first he thought that only his friends were aging, each of his own gray hairs was premature. But now what he had left of his own was stark white. The aches and pains that wracked his limbs were the price of his "glorious football days." He could see where he stood.

> So, I accept, I am resigned.
> I'll let the new rules apply.

But his stoicism went only so far. He continued:

> And sitting there in my rocking chair
> If a 'bikini' passes by
> I'll be circumspect, I promise,
> And look with just one eye.

Chapter 59

When Dr. Eagle died, Valerie took over his practice. She did good business. So did Buzzy Gregory, Dr. Buzzard's son-in-law. There was an epidemic of spiritual affliction, which the doctors and psychiatrists could not understand. "They cannot put themselves down to the level of people who are so possessed. The average psychiatrist hides his head," said McTeer.[245]

"Nobody has any idea of how big this is," he later told an SCETV crew. "I dare say this, there are hundreds of thousands of people from New York City to Albuquerque New Mexico who believe they were under the influence of an evil spell."[246]

A medical technician from the Naval base wrote to McTeer: "I have heard you have extraordinary powers in white witchcraft. If you fail me it will be suicide or insanity for me. Which comes first will be inconsequential." McTeer met the young man, who told him that he had always had an interest in witchcraft and while he was stationed in Beaufort he wanted to meet a root doctor. "Everyone was interested in a mysterious light that was being seen on the Lands End Road at midnight. . . . Groups of young people were making festive parties to witness the phenomena." It was the same light that McTeer had seen that night so many years ago when they were staking out the still.

The young man, whom McTeer called John when he included the story in his next book, said there was a black root doctor claimed to be the "Master of the Light" and took people out to see it. John went with the doctor out to Lands End Road. The unnamed doctor managed to conjure the light up from the swamp. Later, John got chance to talk to the so-called master of the light. "I am a student of the occult and I would like to pay you to help me further my knowledge of this art. . . . I believe

African Witchcraft is the answer to using the astral and kinetic forces." The Doctor told John that if he was serious, he should come over the next night.

John told McTeer, "That was the beginning of my involvement with that man, and now I am living in a perpetual nightmare." He described his apprenticeship to the doctor, how the doctor promised to strengthen his forces. John told McTeer that he saw the root doctor in his sleep each night. His "subconscious mind" could hear the doctor telling him "You are beginning to be afraid of me, John, and you want to quit. But you came to me; I didn't send for you. I need you now in my work; you are very receptive. I don't want the hours I spent with you wasted. So come to me."

McTeer began to treat John. First he made the young man quit smoking marijuana. He performed his ritual and gave him an amulet to keep in his wallet. They corresponded regularly. Eventually, John wrote to McTeer from San Francisco. He reported that was entirely free from the evil doctor's influence.[247]

That case was rare enough for McTeer to include it in the book he was writing about African Witchcraft. But it was only rare because of John's self-awareness. It seemed that someone showed up at Harry's every morning looking for him. He pointed towards the Lafayette building where he had his office. There was an extra room in the back that he set up as his root room; he saw patients there between 9:00 and noon each day.

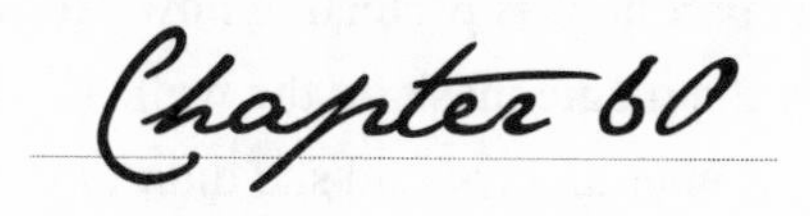

Chapter 60

"I deal in electric emanations of the mind,"[248] McTeer said. "African witchcraft, to me, is the ability to commune with nature and use nature's bounty to bring about desired results."[249] But he needed props. He drove down Highway 21 to the shack on Hunting Island where Driftwood Corey lived. People thought Driftwood Corey was a root doctor, too, and they feared him. He spoke with an Irish brogue. He said he had been wounded in a war, but he never said which one. Roger Pinckney described how Corey "took great chunks of driftwood, trimmed a branch here, rounded a knob there, until they looked like women—naked mostly—then set them like bait along his porch railing. Tourists would slow down and look. Once they slowed, they stopped. Once they stopped, they bought."[250] Corey gave McTeer a "magic mask," an African-looking face painted in bright primary colors on a horseshoe crab shell. He gave the sheriff his mandrake, a piece of driftwood carved to look like a female spirit with horns. McTeer would later tell people that he got the mandrake from Dr. Buzzard. He told them it was three hundred years old. These two artifacts became the focal points in what he would sometimes call his magic act.

He wrote that "to be effective in the practice of witchcraft you must make the person seeking your help believe you have the power to make the astral forces assist you with their problems."[251] It was, in many ways, just like being a sheriff without a gun—you were only as strong as people's belief in you. When asked by the *Charlotte Observer* if he really believed in all this business, he replied, "I'm a believer that I can get into your mind and change your way of thinking. I believe I have enough sensitivity to your brain waves. It's a form of ESP," he said, but then admitted, "Some of it's showbiz, some of it's for real."[252]

It was the showbiz part he was perfecting now. He set up the mandrake on an altar and hung the magic mask on the wall. Thomas McTeer's favorite story: "My mother always said she didn't know how Ed didn't burn the damn place down. He'd keep bags of black gunpowder in his office. He had a secret button under the edge of this table right here, and a wire that ran up behind the posters on the wall. He had two nails and a piece of copper wire tied between them back there behind the mask. And this button was hooked up electrically to 110 volts and he would put a little gun powder under that copper wire and, as he was bringing this whole thing to a crescendo of curative power, he would reach under and hit that button and this thing would blow gunpowder smoke and flame."

Desperate for help, they came to McTeer, white and black alike. A graduate student, Kathryn Heyer, who was writing a dissertation on rootwork on St. Helena, witnessed a case where a middle aged black woman came to see the former sheriff because she felt like snakes were crawling over her shoulders, back and chest. "At one point," Heyer wrote, "she asked the rootworker about the possibility of people being turned into animals, 'like zombies.'" The woman thought her neighbors were jealous of her and that they put a hex on her. She feared she would become a snake zombie.

McTeer told the woman that she had a "clouded aura." He believed evil was involved in troubling her mind and causing the pain. He would help her, he said, but warned that she had to believe in him because he was "putting his reputation on the line for her." McTeer then "filled a small cup with water, asked the woman to dip her fingers in it, placed cardboard over the cup and inverted the whole thing. When he removed the cardboard, the water remained in the cup." McTeer told the woman that "if evil was in fact present some would have gone into the cup. The test, he said, would come from the 'magic mask. . . hanging on the wall. When he moved the cup near the mask there was a tiny explosion and a puff of white smoke came from the mask."[253] That meant the hex was real.

McTeer told the patient to take the tissue and hold it against her neck, where she felt the snakes under her skin. He took the tissue from her. He kept talking as he turned to the table. He twisted the tissue around and took it to another table across the room, which served as a second sort of alter and was covered with wonders and curiosities: Arrowheads, fossils, mastodon bones, and sharks' teeth.

McTeer put his hand on the woman's neck, where she said she felt the snakes. "He explained to the woman that the 'magical forces' from his body were moving into her neck and forcing all the evil into the tissue."[25] Patients reported that they could feel a surge when he touched their shoulders like this.

"Now I go to the mandrake, which is the most powerful thing in here." He struck a match and lit the tissue. He raised it, flaming, above his head, his thick glasses reflecting the flickering light in bright blotches. It was time "to take the evil fully from the person."

There were cardboard boxes filled with old papers on the floor. The wall was the color of medical scrubs. Black shutters were closed against the sunlight and the room smelled like baby powder and muskets. He leaned over the short table and put the tissue in a dish. He picked up the mandrake. "Now I want you to watch," he said, pointing down at the table with one long finger, waving the mandrake with his other hand. "Watch right over there," he instructed. He raised both hands up above his head—a dramatic white flash. That was the evil. "There she goes." He made a gesture like an umpire signaling that a runner is safe in a slow-mo replay. "All the evil is gone," he said waving his hand differently now, in an obvious gesture of benediction.[255]

Finally, he had to make the amulet, or root, for his patient. The amulets were the small squares of blue or red cloth that Lucille, Georgiana, and the other girls sewed for him. Heyer wrote that he held the root in his hand "to put his force into it," then "anointed it with powerful oils, put the stone on top of it, 'to lock in the forces of good,' invoked the mandrake root 'to seal the forces' and finally gave the amulet to the woman." He told her to put it in her bra: "Now this amulet has you and I in it. I've removed all the evil from you."[256]

"I have seen people shaking with fright and after ten or fifteen minutes talking with him they would come out whistling," said Leroy Keyserling.

McTeer told the SCETV crew, "I guess there are fifteen thousand" of his amulets "being carried by women and that many by men."[257]

Chapter 62

McTeer couldn't help everyone who came to him. Heyer witnessed one woman "telling a confused story to the effect that her landlord was raising her rent beyond the amount covered by her welfare check." McTeer asked her who she thought was doing her evil. She "began talking about how her rent was raised again and said that her lights were going to be turned off because her rent payments precluded her paying the light bill." Heyer wrote that McTeer told her "this was not the result of evil forces but was part of the problem of living and due to people's greed. He suggested that she speak with her welfare case worker."[258]

McTeer knew that money was a kind of root. He was planning to include a chapter in his latest book about an eighteenth-century English banking crisis. But he did not tell the patients everything he thought. He knew what his real job was. The doctor "knows you have problems so he listens carefully, trying to find out what is really bothering you."[259] Behind the explosions and the powders and the potions, there was only one man listening to another's problems.

Ed wrote his first three books in three years. But it took him another four to finish his final book, *Fifty Years as a Low Country Witchdoctor*. Writing this book was closely related to his practice. With it, he completed the persona of his new profession. The sheriff was now a full-time root doctor. He found the calling of his final days. Sherwood Fender described McTeer as "almost a waxy white by then. He looked like he never been in the sun. He looked like he'd already been embalmed. And he had long white hair. It really wasn't white, it was a dingy. You seen these old people with white things and they smoke and they get these yellow things that was sort of the color of his hair." He had grown into the part he had always played.

Chapter 63

When Ed's final book came out, things started going badly for L.W. Wallace. The film *Smokey and the Bandit* came out the same year. Wallace bore more than a passing resemblance to the Texas sheriff, Beaufort T. Justice, played by Jackie Gleason. But the real trouble went back to the "Sheriff's Camp" that John Trask had given to the department when Wallace beat McTeer. "Wallace claims that the Trasks had intended that he own the property and the sheriff deeded it to himself in 1971," reported the *Gazette*.[260] He had borrowed money to improve the property and one of his children was living there. He did not intend to let it remain with the department when he left.

When the county found out, they sued.

In the meantime, the council bought the department four radar guns. One of Wallace's political supporters was clocked and ticketed. He complained to Wallace, who took the radar gun from his deputy and threw the fifteen hundred dollar piece of equipment against a wall. Wallace issued an order "asking for all remaining units to be brought to his office."[261]

In September, the grand jury took action against the "sheriff's decision to scuttle his radar units after receiving complaints from his associates who got caught speeding by deputies."

The jury spent "several days" questioning Wallace, his deputies and others involved in the case. Somehow, during this process, Wallace stood up and shoved the grand jury foreman.[262]

Roger Pinckney's father, the coroner, was involved with the whole thing. Roger XI, the writer, told me about it when I went to see him out on Daufuskie Island. "Wallace started suffering some extreme mental problems. And people said that McTeer put the root on him and drove him crazy and Wallace was in court and he reached up and slapped the shit out of the jury foreman who was a retired Marine Brigadier General and went into his house, pulled the phone out of the wall and took his service revolver and sat at the kitchen table.

"So the County Council wrote a letter of resignation and gave it to my daddy to go in and have Wallace sign it. The coroner is the only man who can arrest the sheriff, by law. So Daddy went into the house and Wallace is sitting there with his pistol on the table. He got Wallace to sign the resignation, put Wallace's pistol in his back pocket, and led him out of the house."

Eventually, the Governor would appoint a retired Civil Service worker named Morgan McCutcheon to the job. McTeer did not comment.

Chapter 64

McTeer did not worry much about who succeeded Wallace as sheriff. "The only qualm I have," wrote McTeer at the end of *Fifty Years as a Low Country Witchdoctor*, "is who will succeed me?" McTeer, like Dr. Eagle and Dr. Buzzard before him, wanted to find someone to whom he could say, "I am old, I have things to show you." There were "many, many requirements." The first was practical. The candidate needed to be "virtually retired and financially able and willing to help people."[263]

But there were other, more important, requirements. It was about brain chemistry. "Genetically, your cells should inform you, as your brain develops, if you have been endowed with special gifts. If so the road to your future has been decided for you." He had no choice in either of his careers; the sheriff's blood and the E.S.P. were both genetic. He believed everybody had some level of extrasensory perception, but some were especially equipped to develop it. These people, such as himself, were born with more "highly magnetized brain cells."[264] Most who claimed they wanted to learn were "charlatans . . . who have nothing else to do and have run the gamut with life."[265] He added, "They will not have to tell me; I will know. I only hope it is soon, very soon."[266]

He thought he might pass his mantle on to the graduate student Kathryn Heyer. She reported four training sessions with him, but found that her academic work would not allow her to go any further. She abandoned the apprenticeship.

His granddaughter, Betsy Cooke, approached him one day. She would follow his lead, but go beyond him. She remembered, "He always wanted to go to Africa and when I got out of college I went into the Peace Corps, and I was assigned to Ghana in West Africa. When I first told him I was going to Ghana, he got real silent for a couple of days; I think he was afraid for me, to be honest. But then after that, he called me the night before I left, to say goodbye. My mom said he has never in his life called her. He just didn't reach out to family members like that. But my going to Africa really meant something to him," she said. "I knew when I left my dog would die and granddaddy would die while I was gone and I had to decide that I would go anyway."

Betsy missed her grandfather's last big magic act. State Senator Jimmy Waddell had introduced a bill that would name the new bridge between Lady's Island and Port Royal after McTeer. Construction on the bridge was behind schedule, but McTeer's family pushed to hold the dedication ceremony early. McTeer was in poor health. He had spent years trying to stop the root doctors from practicing medicine without a license, but he would not go to the medical doctor. He told a reporter "regular doctors came from barbers."[267] He would not quit smoking.

They held the dedication in the summer of 1979; Waddell presided as McTeer stood there in a white suit and dark glasses, surrounded by grandchildren and cigarette smoke.

The incomplete bridge reached up for the violent sun with fingers of rust-colored rebar. The state offered McTeer the only immortality it could muster. Waddell said: "It is fitting and indeed appropriate that the memory of this legendary lawman, author, spellbinder and raconteur be kept alive so that posterity may know that in Beaufort County the High Sheriff presided over Camelot with dignity, grace and absolute approbation."

McTeer said every new bridge increased property values, but decreased the isolation of the people. He said that "you had to be half-alligator, half duck to do the job" when he started as sheriff. He acknowledged that "bridges have been the making of Beaufort County," but his words were infected with the elegiac irony that always accompanies memorialization. The bridges that had "made Beaufort" unmade the Beaufort that the name of the bridge was intended to conjure.

It is no accident that such dedications are called *ceremonies*. There is a certain degree of magic in naming. It takes magic to keep the legend of some lost Camelot alive. McTeer was fascinated by root doctors precisely because he saw them as bridges to strange worlds. The coincidence was not lost on Waddell, who acknowledged McTeer's practice as a root doctor in a reference to the reviled "malaise" speech President Jimmy Carter had given the previous evening, suggesting that the old sheriff "put a root on the president to help him restore the confidence of the American people."[268]

McTeer did not cast any spells that day. The heat separated the fabric of the air into a swarm that invaded his eyes. The world went static . . . white.

An ambulance took McTeer to the hospital. They gave him intravenous fluids for exhaustion and dehydration, then released him. He made it to the party in his honor held at Georgiana's house. Betsy could not come home from Africa for the ceremony, but she was thinking of her grandfather. "While I was there I picked up a lot of witchcraft items and sent them back. I was going to Christmas and something told me not to wait and so I went ahead and sent them and he got them before Christmas."

It turned out he needed them.

Chapter 65

When gravediggers discovered a headless corpse in late 1979, the sheriff's office called McTeer. There wasn't much to say about the case, but the reporters came from all over. McTeer performed his ritual for them several times a week.

Ed McTeer was, of course, only a consultant, but he seemed to feel that this case gave him the chance to unite his twin vocations one last time. His friend Leroy Keyserling reported that Ed was in especially good spirits over coffee at Harry's that week. Though it was a cold winter and McTeer was having trouble breathing, he kept smoking. He collapsed again and was brought to the hospital where he died at 7:20 p.m. on 29 December, Georgiana's birthday. He'd suffered from emphysema, pneumonia and "complications of age," but the cause of death was "natural undetermined causes."

McCutcheon had men guard McTeer's corpse. He called McTeer a "real student of human behavior," saying McTeer "could predict when certain kinds of crimes would be committed."[269]

Lucille wore black to the funeral. Little Ed walked beside her, his hand on her shoulder as they followed the grim-faced pallbearers, marching the coffin towards the grave.

Betsy Cooke was not at the funeral. "They didn't try to notify me because it takes too long to get a message across," she explained. "I had a British volunteer staying with me over Christmas. We started talking about granddaddy and his witchcraft and the witchcraft in Ghana and I told her . . . I said, 'For some reason I feel like he's gone.' I don't know why but in my heart I felt like he was gone. This was New Year's Eve. And I got the first letter that came some time after that. I was in a staff meeting and I opened it and it started out 'My dearest Betsy, I'm so sorry to say. . .' and I just folded it up and got up and walked out of the meeting, because I knew exactly what it said. Somehow I had already known he was gone."

Thomas McTeer recalled after the funeral his "mother wanted to destroy everything because she was afraid that people would try to get it or use it or mock it or whatever. My wife and I were the designated correspondence answerers after his death and we spent about a year doing nothing but emptying out his mail box once a day and answering the letters and sending people their locks of hair back and fingernails. That and going down and cleaning his grave off. That was always a real pain because people for a long time after that would come burn incense, sprinkle white powder around it, and take dirt off it."

Ed McTeer died before he found a successor. And yet, as the bridge that bears his name turns thirty, everyone who knew him practices his art. They use McTeer as the bridge to connect them to the strangest of worlds—the past. They become animated when they speak of him: they summon him, imbibe his sheriff's blood, and bring back his ghost.

It gets harder every year to imagine the world that made McTeer's life possible. The population of Beaufort has again doubled in the years since his death. "I don't know what he'd think about our world," his son Ed told me, standing in the kitchen of his Coffin Point home, in front of a grandchild's drawing of a Japanese cartoon character, hanging on the refrigerator door. "I just can't imagine him with a cell phone."

Sheriff McTeer was a man of his time, but he transcended it. For us, he is a bridge to a dissolving past. In his own day, he was a link to an unforeseen future. I went to see Cleaver Johnson, the former President of the NAACP, on the fortieth anniversary of the March on Washington, the historic event that had been planned barely a mile from where we sat. Johnson had always believed McTeer was an ally in the fight for justice. "Mr. McTeer had black people like his friend," he said, sitting there that day in his living room, on No Man's Land Road, halfway between Coffin Point and the Penn Center, waiting to watch Barack Obama accept the Presidential nomination of the Democratic Party.

"You ain't got many people alive that know 'bout McTeer. Like my son in there," he said pointing at the man in the adjoining kitchen. "He forty-eight years old and he don't know nothing 'bout no McTeer."

"There's the McTeer Bridge," his son corrected him.

"There *is* the McTeer Bridge," the elder Johnson agreed, leaning forward in his chair, surrounded by the past and waiting for the future. "There is that."

Epilogue

The case of the beheaded corpse was never solved. "And, that's not a cold case we're about to reopen," said Neil Baxley of the current sheriff's office.

I came to think about the case again when I met Stephaney Robinson's grandson, whom I'll call Dr. B. He used his name, but I will not. Root doctors are not like psychics with bright signs set up on the side of the road. "It's kind of a secret society. You have to be introduced," Grace Cordial of the Beaufort County Library told me.

Roger Pinckney had introduced me and I set up an appointment. Dr. B told me where to go, and it was the same plantation Stephaney Robinson had lived on. Buzzy was Stephaney Robinson's chosen successor; he'd married the great root doctor's daughter, but was not Buzzard's blood kin. Dr. B. was.

I turned off Highway 21. It was high tide and the marsh stretched out around the road, spiked with spooky old oaks. The sky was still, the spring day sharp. I noticed a woman standing beside the road in all white. She was staring off at the water rustling with cord grass in the wind. She did not turn to look at me. The wind fluttered through her robes, a searing brightness against the flaxen ground. She looked like a ghost.

I saw the buzzards circling over the place where I was headed. As instructed, I pulled up in front of two gray outbuildings and called Dr. B from my cell phone.

A man got off a blue tractor in the distance. A moment later, he walked out from between the two buildings. One of them had broken windows and old school desks inside. We shook hands. He was a tremendous man with a bald head that was twice as big as my own. His face was fleshy, his eyes set deep. We walked around the first building and stood at the door of the second, marked by a sign that bore his name. He opened it and motioned me in. I entered. It smelled like incense and baby powder "It's dark," he said, his voice deep and heavy. "But it will get lighter."

I wasn't sure I believed him. He gestured towards the couch. I sat down.

"What's bothering you? Bad luck? Pains?"

"I'm writing about Ed McTeer," I said. "And I'm a little worried. It's kind of like bringing someone back from the dead when you write about them. And your grandfather…I don't want to offend any spirits or anything."

He laughed. Then he told me a root would cost three hundred dollars. "I'll prepare it for you and then you really shouldn't even let anyone else touch it. You might not know who your enemies are. They could neutralize it."

"I'm sorry," I said. "But whatever else I may be afraid of, I'm more afraid of my wife if I spend three hundred dollars in the middle of a recession."

"I understand," he said, smiling. Then he gave me the root I was really after and started to talk about Ed McTeer.

"Sheriff McTeer said he defeated my grandfather. He talked a lot about things he didn't know anything about. When that body got beheaded, they come around and talk to everybody, asking what it was about. Nobody said anything except for McTeer, and he died the next day—the very next day. He talked about things you don't talk about."

I thanked him and got up to leave. He gave me two business cards. He opened the door, but we paused there in the threshold. A triangle of sun shone on our feet. "Don't worry," Dr. B. assured me. "You can't reveal anything that would hurt you." His words hung in an ominous silence, before he added, "You'll never know enough."

Acknowledgments:

This book was born out of the stories people tell and I have accumulated tremendous debts to all the people—both living and dead—who have shared their stories with me. Their stories give the book strength—any weaknesses are mine alone.

I would like to thank the McTeer family, especially Thomas and Ed. Betsy Cooke and Lucy McDowall were also especially helpful. The book wouldn't exist without Richard and Susan Woods, who first gave me McTeer's books and introduced me to Sherwood Fender, who set everything in motion with great gusto. I hope that something of Sherwood's spirit infuses this story. Roger Pinckney has been a tremendous help and a true friend. Harry Chakides, Joe Mix, Marvin Dukes, and the Paul brothers were all fascinating and generous with their time and memories. Cleaver Johnson also displayed tremendous generosity—and, like those I've just listed, deserves a story in his own right. Pierre McGowan treated me to his boundless energy and enthusiasm reminiscent of Sheriff McTeer. Lieutenant Governor Brantley Harvey was both charming and wise. Agent Danny March enlivened the book with his memories. Lt. Col. Neil Baxley of the Beaufort County Sheriff's Office was an invaluable resource and an excellent researcher who gave the book far greater depth than it would have otherwise had. Grace Cordial, of the Beaufort Room at the County Library, was brilliant and lived up to both of her names. The Penn Center was extremely helpful at providing context, as were Marquetta Goodwine and Alexia Helsley. Arnold Gregory is the real deal. Joe Formicella, Suzanne Hudson, and Shari Smith all believed in the book—believed in me— and they convinced others to take a chance. I am forever grateful to them and to Clay Risen for insisting I go to Fairhope with him. Damien Ober provided invaluable perspectives and support and Katherine Broadway did a whole lot more than copy edit—she was the hammer that helped kill useless words. Lawrence Weschler helped me find the beginning. I'd like to thank my editor Jim Gilbert and the whole team at River City. My parents, John and Martha Woods, deserve a great deal of credit for filling me with a love of stories and putting up with a lot of nonsense. Frances-Earle keeps me well grounded and well fed. Eamon, Jeff, and all the other guys I pick with have taught me so much about rhythm and layering over the years and I hope the spirit of the Dueling Creek Playboys and Jerry Lee Atwater have made their way into the music of the book. Paige Williams, James Wallace, and Jack Lunan gave me an early education. Charles Steen helped me set my sights. Many of my students have taught me more than I've taught them, especially those at Chavez. Gertrude Woods, Carl Summey, and Mike King have all passed on, but there is something of each of them in this book. I am most grateful to my wife, Nicole King. She inspires and challenges me every day and makes me a far better man than I could otherwise hope to be. She encouraged me to take a big chance—and backed me up on it. She shared an office with me and put up with loud typing, crazy voodoo maps, and ghosts wandering the room. She was literally beside me the whole time, writing her own book. That's as good as it gets. This is book's for you, Skeet.

Notes

1 Michael Ludden, "Body unearthed, head cut off in voodoo right," *Beaufort Gazette*, December 4, 1979.
2 Ken Allen, "Lowcountry voodoo?" *Charlotte Observer*, *McTeer Scrapbook,* Beaufort Room, Beaufort County Library.
3 McTeer, *Fifty Years as a Low Country Witchdoctor, 24.*
4 Michael Ludden, "Removal of head may be step in ritual," *Beaufort Gazette,* December 5, 1979.
5 McTeer, *Beaufort Now and Then*, 110
6 Ibid.
7 Ibid.
8 Ibid., 111.
9 Ibid., 140.
10 Ibid.,112.
11 McTeer, *High Sheriff of the Low Country,* 18.
12 McTeer, *Fifty Years,* 13.
13 Ibid.
14 McTeer, *Beaufort*, 139.
15 McTeer, *Fifty Years*, 15.
16 Lynne Katonak, "Voodoo Alive and Well in S.C. Lowcountry," *Aiken Standard,* February 7, 1978. *McTeer Scrapbook.*
17 Ronald Daise, "Marine may be thankful to be free of evil," *Beaufort Gazette*, November 21, 1979.
18 McTeer, *Fifty Years*, 16.
19 Ibid.
20 Ibid., 17.
21 McTeer, *Beaufort*, 138.
22 McTeer, *Beaufort,* 140.
23 Hemingway, *The Complete Short Stories,* 111.
24 McTeer, *Beaufort,* 140.
25 Ibid.,124.

26 "Leroy Kyserling," *High Sheriff, Low Country Witch Doctor*, SCETV, DVD
27 McTeer, *Beaufort*, 101.
28 http://www.youtube.com/watch?v=h9E7T2GtI0w
29 http://www.bge.com/portal/site/bge/menuitem.dcdb00ae9edeb438ec8f1457025166a0/
30 Jim Littlejohn, "J.E. McTeer, Wizard of Land's End." *Islander of Hilton Head Island*, July 1974.
31 Mencken, "Sahara of the Bozart," *A Mencken Chrestomathy*, 134.
32 W.M. Watkins, "J.E. McTeer, Sheriff Without a Gun," *Sandlapper*, April 1968, 18.
33 Jim Littlejohn, "J.E. McTeer, Wizard of Land's End," *Islander of Hilton Head Island*, July 1974, 37.
34 McTeer, *High Sheriff*, 1.
35 "Visits jail and chaingang," *Beaufort Gazette*, July 22, 1926.
36 McTeer, *High Sheriff*, 19.
37 "Kill each other Saturday night," *Beaufort Gazette,* March 11, 1926.
38 McTeer, *Beaufort,* 126.
39 Ibid.
40 "Candidates for sheriff," *Beaufort Gazette*, August 26, 1926.
41 McTeer, *High Sheriff*, 20.
42 "Beaufort Sheriff Expert on Voodoo," *McTeer Scrapbook.*
43 McTeer, *High Sheriff*, 79.
44 McTeer, *Fifty Years,* 22.
45 McTeer, *High Sheriff*, 1.
46 McTeer, *High Sheriff*, 4.
47 Ibid.
48 Jim Littlejohn, "Wizard of Land's End," *Islander of Hilton Head Island*, July, 1974.
49 "Randolph Murdaugh" *High Sheriff, Lowcountry Witch Doctor*, SCETV, DVD.
50 McTeer, *High Sheriff*, 72.
51 "Negro shot by officers," *Beaufort Gazette*, November 4, 1926.
52 McTeer, *High Sheriff*, 82.
53 Pinkney, *Blue Roots*, 94.
54 Long, *Spiritual Merchants*, 93.
55 Hyatt, *Hoodoo Vol. 2,* 2092.

56 Ibid.

57 Long, *Spiritual Merchants*, 95.

58 "Ms. Lupo weds J.E. McTeer," *Beaufort Gazette*, June 9, 1927.

59 Ibid.

60 "Shot down by negroes while attempting to make an arrest," *Beaufort Gazette*, June 9, 1927.

61 "Crime wave," *Beaufort Gazette*, June 23, 1927.

62 "Militia companies guard negroes," *Beaufort Gazette*, June 30, 1927.

63 "Officers not taking chances," *Beaufort Gazette*, June 30, 1927.

64 Bob Flanagan, "McTeer taken ill after bridge dedication," *Carolina News,* July 17, 1979.

65 McTeer, *High Sheriff*, 65.

66 "Negro assaults white woman Saturday near Hardeeville," Beaufort Gazette, July 14, 1927; McTeer, *High Sheriff*, 66.

67 McTeer, *High Sheriff,* 64.

68 Ibid.

69 Ibid.

70 Ibid.

71 Ibid.

72 "Notice of appeal saves negroes," *Beaufort Gazette,* August 11, 1927

73 McTeer, High Sheriff, 92.

74 McTeer, *High Sheriff,* 1.

75 *McTeer Scrapbook.*

76 "Negroes lose appeal in murder case," *Beaufort Gazette*, January 31, 1929.

77 "Body of negro woman found in marsh husband held for committing crime," *Beaufort Gazette*, January, 31, 1929.

78 McTeer, *High Sheriff,* 101.

79 "Big liquor haul made by officers," *Beaufort Gazette*, January 17, 1929.

80 *Beaufort Gazette*, February 28, 1929.

81 "Beaufort County Board of Directors," *Beaufort Gazette*, April 4, 1929.

82 McTeer, *High Sheriff*, 1.

83 McTeer, *High Sheriff,* 14.

84 "Liquor, men and automobiles captured last Wednesday by Sheriff and deputies," *Beaufort Gazette*, August 15, 1929

85 McTeer, *High Sheriff*, 14.

86 “Liquor, men and automobiles captured last Wednesday by Sheriff and deputies,” *Beaufort Gazette*, August 15, 1929

87 Ibid.

88 “Kit Singleton badly beaten,” *Beaufort Gazette*, August 8, 1929; “Unable to identify his assailants,” *Beaufort Gazette*, September 5, 1929.

89 “Slayers of Langford escape chair—will not die,” *Beaufort Gazette*, October 26, 1929.

90 “Beaufort men answer call in flooded section,” *Beaufort Gazette*, October 17, 1929.

91 Ibid.

92 Ibid.

93 Ibid.

94 Ibid.

95 Ibid.

96 “Sheriff McTeer uses fist on drunken marine to get him under control,” *Beaufort Gazette*, November 21, 1929.

97 Ibid.

98 Ibid.

99 Ibid.

100 Adams, “Dr. Bug, Dr. Buzzard and the U.S.A.,” *True,* July, 1949. Beaufort County Library, Dr. Buzzard knoll.

101 “Joe Rivers now in jail,” *Beaufort Gazette,* January 16, 1930.

102 Ibid.

103 Ibid.

104 “Big jail delivery nipped in the bud by officers just at right time,” *Beaufort Gazette*, June 5, 1930.

105 “Officers get two men and liquor,” *Beaufort Gazette*, April 24, 1930.

106 McTeer, *High Sheriff*, 6.

107 Ibid., 7.

108 Ibid.

109 “Sheriff captures boat, liquor and crew five men,” *Beaufort Gazette*, September 25, 1930.

110 “Harry Boyle was arrested Monday,” *Beaufort Gazette*, November 16, 1930.

111 Ibid.

112 "Carden slayer captured for Sheriff here," *Beaufort Gazette*, February 4, 1932.

113 "Sheriff McTeer brought Willie Heyward back from Pittsburgh," *Beaufort Gazette*, February 11, 1932; "Beaufort prisoner pleads not guilty," *Beaufort Gazette*, February 18, 1932.

114 McTeer, *Adventure*, 36.

115 Ibid.

116 McTeer, *High Sheriff,* 84.

117 http://www.scpronet.com/point/9509/s03.html, Edited and reprinted with permission from *Nude and Natural*, the magazine of the Naturist Society.

118 *McTeer Scrapbook.*

119 http://www.scpronet.com/point/9509/s03.html

120 McTeer, *High Sheriff*, 85.

121 "A Merciful Sheriff," *McTeer Scrapbook.*

122 McTeer, *Beaufort*, 102.

123 Ibid.

124 "Three men arrested for stealing meat from the relief warehouse," *Beaufort Gazette*, April 5, 1934.

125 Ibid.

126 Ibid.

127 McTeer, *High Sheriff*, 70.

128 "Two lunatics arrested," *Beaufort Gazette,* November 2, 1933.

129 "Thief caught by Sheriff McTeer," *Beaufort Gazette*, November 9, 1933.

130 McTeer, *High Sheriff*, 85-86.

131 McKelway and Liebling, "Who is this King of Glory," *New Yorker,* June 13, 1936.

132 McTeer, *Fifty Years*, 10.

133 Ibid.

134 McTeer, *Fifty Years,* 28.

135 Linda Caughman, "Former Beaufort Sheriff known as Low Country Witch Doctor," *The State*, November 16, 1972; McTeer Scrapbook.

136 McTeer, *Fifty Years*, 43.

137 Ibid., 104.

138 McTeer, *High Sheriff*, 28.

139 Ibid.

140 Ibid.

141 "Sheriff J.E. McTeer purchases Odell Home," *Beaufort Gazette*, July 28, 1938.

142 McTeer, *Beaufort,* 126.

143 Ibid., 127.

144 "Mrs. J.E. McTeer buried Wednesday," *Beaufort Gazette*, January 26, 1939.

145 McTeer, *Adventure*, 37

146 Ibid.

147 Ibid., 38.

148 Ibid.

149 Ibid.

150 Ibid.

151 "Sheriffs vigorously oppose state police plan; form committee to advise drafters," *McTeer Scrapbook.*

152 "Ben Heyward captured in Ohio—Killed Paul Carden in 1925," *Beaufort Gazette,* October 12, 1939.

153 McTeer, *Adventure*, 39.

154 "Ceballos returns for War Bond allotment task," *McTeer Scrapbook.*

155 "Coast Guard sluggers, having won here now head for Golden Gloves," *News and Courier, McTeer Scrapbook.*

156 Doug Donehue "Man on a Lonely Beach," *News and Courier, McTeer Scrapbook.*

157 "Beaufort plans big Navy Day Celebration on October 27," *McTeer Scrapbook.*

158 Samuel Hopkins Adams, "Dr. Bug, Dr. Buzzard, and the U.S.A.," *True Magazine,* June 1949.

159 McTeer, *High Sheriff*, 24.

160 Adams, "Dr. Bug," *True*, 70.

161 Ibid.

162 Ibid.

163 Ibid.

164 Doug Donehue, "Man on a Lonely Beach," *News and Courier, McTeer Scrapbook.*

165 Adams, "Dr. Bug," *True*, 71.

166 Ibid.

167 Ibid.

168 Adams, "Dr. Bug," *True*, 71.

169 Pinckney, *Blue Roots*, 58.

170 McTeer, *High Sheriff*, 23.

171 "Randolph Murdaugh," *High Sheriff, Lowcountry Witch Doctor*, SCETV, DVD.

172 McTeer, *High Sheriff*, 23.

173 McTeer, *Fifty Years*, 24.

174 Ibid.

175 Pinckney, *Blue Roots*, 104.

176 Ken Allen, "Former sheriff fights witchcraft with white magic," *Charlotte Observer,* December 15, 1979.

177 Rob Wood, "Witchcraft Lives," Associated Press*, McTeer Scrapbook.*

178 McTeer, *Fifty Years*, 25.

179 Ronald Daise, "Marine may be thankful to be free of evil." *Beaufort Gazette,* November 21, 1979.

180 McTeer, *High Sheriff*, 21.

181 "S.C. ghost passes up experts," *News and Observer*, October 29, 1972.

182 Bass, and Thompson, *Strom*, 80.

183 *McTeer Scrapbook.*

184 McTeer, *Fifty Years,* 37.

185 "Gives boy to the sheriff," *McTeer Scrapbook.*

186 Bass and Thompson, *Strom*, 102.

187 "S.C. Sheriffs back Thurmond," *McTeer Scrapbook.*

188 "Plantation turnover growing larger," *McTeer Scrapbook.*

189 "Leroy Keyserling," High Sheriff, Lowcountry Witch Doctor, SCETV, DVD.

190 Cattleman seized as slayer of socialite," *The News,* February 20, 1949.

191 "Whiskey glass is Swain clue," *McTeer Scrapbook.*

192 "S.C. Youths test 'First H-Bomb; Results are Drastic," *Associated Press*, December 14, 1950, *McTeer Scrapbook.*

193 "Committee named to study primary," *Beaufort Gazette,* July 28, 1949.

194 "Two week itinerary opens at Barrel Landing Tues," *Beaufort Gazette,* June 30, 1950

195 *Beaufort Gazette*, July 6, 1950.

196 "Second race seen in doubt; McTeer returned as sheriff," *Beaufort Gazette,* July 20, 1950.

197 Ibid.

198 McTeer, *High Sheriff*, 49.
199 McTeer, *High Sheriff*, 45-46.
200 McTeer, *High Sheriff*, 39-40.
201 *McTeer Scrapbook.*
202 McTeer, *Beaufort*, 141-142.
203 *McTeer Scrapbook.*
204 "Six negro men are jailed in death of 'Human Torch,'" *Beaufort Gazette,* February 19, 1959.
205 "Two wounded Saturday as pistols find targets," *Beaufort Gazette,* March 5, 1959.
206 "Husband strikes again at Coosaw Island wife," *Beaufort Gazette*, March 26, 1959.
207 "40-year-old killing ends in arrest of hunted man," *Beaufort Gazette*, April 30, 1959.
208 "Storm compared to A-Bomb by Beaufort victim," *News and Courier*, *McTeer Scrapbook.*
209 Helsley, *Beaufort, South Carolina: A History*, 195.
210 McTeer, Beaufort, *141.*
211 Ibid.
212 McTeer, *High Sheriff*, 35.
213 "Two negroes wounded in blazing gun battle," *Beaufort Gazette*, February 18, 1960.
214 McTeer, *Fifty Years,* 79.
215 "McTeer Agency sold to People's," *Beaufort Gazette,* February 2, 1961.
216 "Stanley offering voters 'choice' in sheriff's race," *Beaufort Gazette*, June 7, 1962.
217 Ibid.
218 "Field of candidates for sheriff is now firmed up at three," *Beaufort Gazette,* September 1962.
219 "In Sheriff's Race: Wallace Candidate; Bessinger is Out," *Beaufort Gazette*, October 18, 1962.
220 Pinckney, *Blue Roots*, 107.
221 "Candidates file expenditures in general election," *Beaufort Gazette*, November 15, 1962.
222 Helsley, *Beaufort*, 204.
223 "Sheriff Decision Coming Tuesday," *Beaufort Gazette*, November 8, 1962.

224 “Sheriff race hearing granted for Friday,” *Beaufort Gazette,* November 15, 1962.

225 “Sheriff’s race ‘null and void,’” *Beaufort Gazette*, November 22, 1962.

226 “Only one name on ballot for new election: Governor orders re-run on Dec. 11,” *Beaufort Gazette*, November 29, 1962.

227 Pinckney, *Blue Roots,* 107-108.

228 “Sheriff election is coming Tuesday,” *Beaufort Gazette,* December 6, 1962.

229 “Heavy vote puts Wallace in Office,” *Beaufort Gazette*, December 13, 1962.

230 Ibid.

231 McTeer, *Fifty Years*, 37.

232 Ibid.,38.

233 McTeer, “If I had my way,” *Adventure.*

234 McTeer, “The Vacant Chair,” *Adventure.*

235 Monica Maria Tetzlaff, “The Penn Center, the Penn School, and Friends,” *Friends Journal,* March 1997.

236 Shaila Dewan, “Through trying times for blacks, a place of peace,” *New York Times*, April 4, 2008.

237 McTeer, *High Sheriff*, 101.

238 McTeer, *High Sheriff*, 32.

239 McTeer, *High Sheriff*, 33-37.

240 Ibid.,iv.

241 Ibid.,31

242 “Historian, ex-sheriff briefs Marines,” *News and Courier*, August 19, 1971.

243 McTeer, *Fifty Years,* 37.

244 McTeer, *Fifty Years,* 83.

245 Mark Pinsky, “High Sheriff of the Low Country,” *Facing South, McTeer Scrapbook.*

246 *High Sheriff, Lowcountry Witch Doctor*, SCETV, DVD.

247 McTeer, *Fifty Years,* 69-71.

248 Ibid.,39.

249 Ibid.,45.

250 Pinckney, “The Moon in Three Phases,” *Signs and Wonders*,1.

251 McTeer, *Fifty Years*, 82.

252 Ken Allen, "Former sheriff fights witchcraft with white magic," *Charlotte Observer*, December 15, 1979.

253 Heyer, *Rootwork*, 115.

254 Ibid.

255 *High Sheriff, Lowcountry Witchdoctor*, SCETV, DVD.

256 Heyer, *Rootwork,* 115.

257 *High Sheriff, Lowcountry Witchdoctor*, SCETV, DVD.

258 Heyer, *Rootwork*, 117.

259 McTeer, *High Sheriff*, 31.

260 Thomas Westbury, "County, Sheriff land tiff," *Beaufort Gazette*, July 29, 1977.

261 "Wallace cans all four radar units," *Beaufort Gazette*, September 2, 1977.

262 "Grand jury ponders taking action," *Beaufort Gazette*, September 16, 1977.

263 McTeer, *Fifty Years,* 104.

264 McTeer, *Fifty Years*, 102.

265 Nancy Roberts, "White Witch Doctor of the Low Country," *The Faces of South Carolina*, 56.

266 McTeer, Fifty Years, 105.

267 *McTeer Scrapbook.*

268 Bob Flanagan, "McTeer taken ill after bridge dedication," *Carolina News*, July 17, 1979.

269 William Whitten, "S.C. Lawman McTeer dies," *Evening Post*, December 30, 1979, *McTeer Scrapbook.*

Bibliography

Archival Sources

Beaufort Collection, Beaufort County Library, South Carolina
McTeer Scrapbook.
Dr. Buzzard, a knoll.

Newspapers
Associated Press
Beaufort Gazette. Beaufort, South Carolina.
Charleston News and Courier. Charleston, South Carolina.
Charlotte Observer. Charlotte, North Carolina.
News and Observer, Raleigh, North Carolina.
New York Times. New York, New York.
State. Columbia, South Carolina.

Other sources
Adams, "Dr. Bug, Dr. Buzzard and the U.S.A.," True, July, 1949. Beaufort County Library, Dr. Buzzard knoll.

Bass, Jack and Marjorie Thompson. Strom: The Complicated Personal and Political Life of Strom Thurmond. New York: Public Affairs, 2005.

Baxandall, Lee. "Baring Witness," Nude and Natural, the magazine of the Naturist Society, 1995. http://www.scpronet.com/point/9509/s03.html

Helsley, Alexia Jones. Beaufort, South Carolina: A History. Charleston: History Press, 2005.

Hemingway, Ernest. "Soldier's Home," The Complete Short Stories of Ernest Hemingway. New York: Simon and Schuster, 1987

Heyer, Kathryn Wilson, Rootwork: Psychosocial Aspects of Malign Magical Illness Beliefs in a South Carolina Sea Island Community. Dissertation, Department of Sociology, University of Connecticut, 1981.

Jim Littlejohn, "J.E. McTeer, Wizard of Land's End." Islander of Hilton Head Island, July 1974.

McGowan, Pierre. The Gullah Mailman. Pentland: Raleigh, 2000.

McTeer, J.E. Adventure in the Woods and Waters of the Low Country. Beaufort: Beaufort Book Co., 1972.

---- Beaufort Now and Then. Columbia: R.L. Bryan, 1971.

----Fifty Years as a Low Country Witch Doctor. Columbia: R.L. Bryan, 1976.

----High Sheriff of the Low Country, Columbia, R.L. Bryan, 1970.

H.L. Mencken, The American Scene: A Reader. New York: Knopf, 1977.

Pinckney, Roger. Blue Roots: African American Folk Magic of the Gullah People. Orangeburg: Sandlapper, 2003.

---- Little Glory. Wyreck, 2003.

---- Signs and Wonders. Charleston, Wyreck, 2004.

Roberts, Nancy "White Witch Doctor of the Low Country," The Faces of South Carolina. Garden City, NY: Doubleday, 1976.

SCETV. High Sheriff, Low Country Witch Doctor, Beaufort, DVD

Tetzlaff, Monica Marie. "The Penn Center, the Penn School, and Friends," *Friends Journal,* March 1997

W.M. Watkins, "J.E. McTeer, Sheriff Without a Gun," Sandlapper, April 1968